FOLLY or POWER?

FOLLY or POWER?

Encounter Groups in the Church

STANLEY C. BROWN

and

ROBERT H. DEITS

HAWTHORN BOOKS, INC.
W. Clement Stone, Publisher
New York

FOLLY OR POWER?

Library of Congress Catalog Card Number: 74-22919
ISBN: 0-8015-2732-5
1 2 3 4 5 6 7 8 9 10

CONTENTS

In Appreciation

How do you say thank you to friends, especially those with whom you have shared some of life's deepest feelings? Words pale in meaning; simple appreciation sounds corny. Yet, we are grateful to so many.

Our wives are at the top of the list. They not only shared this pilgrimage with us, but also encouraged us to write it down—even when that meant less time with them.

Then there are our congregations, who endured our growing pains (and still do), and, of course, the groups themselves. To those friends who recognize their stories in the text (under assumed names), thanks for letting us share.

To Bonnie Flickinger, who typed the original manuscript long before we ever knew it would be published—our special gratitude.

Virginia Shaw helped in a special way with several portions of the manuscript.

Now we reach out to touch and thank all who enter these pages with us. May our folly be power to you.

THE AUTHORS

FOLLY or POWER?

Introduction

For the word of the cross is folly to those who are perishing, but to us who are being saved it is the power of God. (I Corinthians 1:18)

Folly or Power? is the account of a spiritual pilgrimage by the two authors. Beginning from widely divergent backgrounds and levels of involvement in the church, both of us were drawn into the stream of the small-group movement. Sometimes eagerly, often unwillingly, we each followed a separate path in various types of small groups both in and out of the local church. Increasingly, our experiences as ministers convinced us that we were in touch with something important and exciting. We were seeing the signs of the kingdom of God: people imprisoned by fear and anxiety were released to new life—impoverished personalities were enriched with good news to share—broken victims of life were stretching their souls in sudden freedom.

When our separate pilgrimages merged, our concerns and convictions had become so similar that we became a team. We soon concluded that the style of small groups known as "encounter groups" offered the best possibility for the Christian church in our time. We need to say at the outset that the word *encounter* has a deep spiritual dimension for us. It means *meeting*—meeting each other in openness, honesty, and trust. This meeting each other has the same character as our meeting God. We are convinced that only in such meeting will new life be born and growth take place.

Folly or Power? has been written primarily from an experiential point of view. We want to tell you what happened to us, what we tried in our groups, how it worked, and how we feel about it.

We are not offering here a "last word" on how to lead encounter groups—although we do offer some ground rules, suggestions for starting groups, and specific ways in which the Christian life can be enriched using the principles of encounter. In Appendix 1 are some "group games" which enable persons to dramatize and understand their feelings. Appendix 2 is a description of an encounter workshop, which is a good way to introduce encounter groups to people.

One of the things we've become aware of most keenly is the power of the encounter group and the tremendous potential for good that exists as persons move beyond superficiality and start exploring their inner selves. Likewise, experts in the field point out that an element of danger exists if a poorly trained or improperly motivated leader is in charge. That is why we emphasize the importance of leadership training and why we have made an effort to inform the reader of various opportunities and resources that are available. While we believe *Folly or Power?* to be a significant resource, it is not a substitute for personal training. If encounter groups have as much potential value as it would seem, surely it is worth a leader's time and energy to acquire as much skill as possible.

Terminology defined

Because the terms used in the small-group movement cover such a broad spectrum of meaning, we want to make clear what we mean in this book by certain words.

An *encounter group* is a small number of "normal" people who meet together at least weekly for a minimum of one and one-half hours for the purpose of experiencing (getting to know) each other in feelings, behavior, attitudes, and responses in the here and now. (Although *normal* is difficult to define, we use it to denote persons who are free of any serious and crippling emotional problems.) The word *encounter* indicates a dimension of depth in the interaction between persons in the group. It is not a casual social gathering, but one which has impact upon the participants. Their interaction is characterized by openness, loving honesty, acceptance, risking, and testing. We believe the principle of encounter has a definite spiritual base. The profound I-Thou encounter between people (as opposed to I-It) is analogous to the I-Thou encounter between God and man.

Group games, as described in this book, are certain techniques which help persons dramatize internal feelings (thus getting them out front, where they can be dealt with openly), and facilitate interaction in the group. Games can enliven the group and help it through inevitable "flat" spots.

These terms should not be confused with, nor taken as synonymous with, the extreme kinds of short-term groups and group activities currently popular in some areas of society. Neither should they be understood as just another form of prayer-and-share group. What we unashamedly offer is both Christ-centered and person-centered.

Because most of what we share here has evolved from personal experience and not from theory, we have found it necessary to speak often in the first person singular. Perhaps this is appropriate for a book dealing with openness and honesty in personal relationships.

Since coauthorship could lead to some confusion as to the identity of the person(s) speaking, we adopted this format: when one of us has written for both, the name of the writer comes first—for example, "Stan and Bob" at the beginning of a chapter indicates that Stan wrote it for both of us. If we wrote a chapter individually, one name will appear at the beginning.

We sincerely hope that what we have written from our experiences will be both practical and helpful.

PART ONE

"Consider Your Call"

For consider your call, brethren; not many of you were wise according to worldly standards, not many were powerful, not many were of noble birth. . . (I Corinthians 1:26)

Chapter 1

□

Called to Search
(The Discovery)

STAN BROWN:

The windmills in the surrounding fields looked very strange to my wife, Ruth, and me when we landed in Palma de Mallorca. Though they seemed to come straight out of *Don Quixote*, they were no figment of our imaginations, and neither was the giant we met in the person of Paul Tournier. Two hundred Americans, all active in various kinds of church renewal efforts, had come together in Spain for a seminar with this leader of practical psychology whose books have deeply affected so many lives.

Someone has called Tournier "walking love." It is true. We didn't need an interpreter to receive his message about human relationships. He had no system to teach, no outline on how to be a good counselor, no rules of thumb. He simply shared his own spiritual pilgrimage. Tournier was real, open, and genuine, not afraid to be vulnerable or "unprofessional." His love for people was admittedly anchored in Jesus Christ, though he felt no compulsion to convert those who came to him. He only desired to "invite them to himself."

What an unforgettable phrase!

He told us of his childhood as an orphan, and how utterly lonely his life was. Then a Greek teacher, an atheist sensitive to Tournier's isolation, invited the youth to his office just to talk. He was the only person who really cared that the boy was lonely, and Tournier described what happened with those beautiful words, "He invited me to himself!"

Thus, a personal relationship with an atheist introduced Paul Tournier to the presence and love of God. Years later the psychologist asked his Greek teacher to approve the manuscript of his first book. As they sat together in the familiar way, the teacher asked Tournier to read the first chapter to him. The author did so and waited for some reaction.

"Read another chapter."

Again he read and waited, but the request was to read on. So, through the hours, Tournier read out loud, and when he finished there was silence. Finally the teacher said, "Would you lead me in prayer?"

Startled, Tournier asked, "When did you become a believer?"

His old friend answered, "Just now!"

Ripples of confirmation swept over me as I listened to this story, for I, too, had found that the real doorway into the presence of God is through long-term, trust-filled human relationships. The two hundred laymen and pastors on that retreat echoed this fundamental discovery, for we were all persons involved in small, personal-growth groups—in cities and small towns, in congregations and neighborhoods, in company offices and in plants, in community programs.

This was in February, 1970. My mind went back across twelve years of searching for a style of ministry which the Holy Spirit could use most effectively in our time—a style that would put me in partnership with him. Over the months one answer emerged: small groups.

The answer first proved significant in my pastoral counseling experiences. Most of the persons who came with emotional troubles were unable to experience love. They were caught in that vicious cycle of rejection, anger, and guilt which perpetuates itself in a descending spiral. I would ask them to describe God as they experienced him, and after much hesitancy, the picture would emerge as either a vague blur or a wrathful disciplinarian. Neither understanding of God allowed for a personal relationship of love.

Clearly, their relationship with some human being was the key to therapy, to meaning in life, and to the discovery of a relationship with God as he is understood in Jesus Christ. I found that if these troubled persons learned to trust me, whom they could see, it was a stepping stone to trusting God, whom they could not see. Being together hour after hour over the weeks was the framework in which we built a mutual trust and mediated the love of God to each other.

I slowly learned how to be a real person with those who came to me, not a professional counselor so much as a friend. I accepted them as they were, but I also allowed myself the luxury of being human in our relationship by sharing my own real feelings and admitting my weaknesses. I didn't hesitate to let these persons know that I needed to be needed and they were helping me.

Learning to trust takes time, and I didn't have enough time for everyone. Pastoral counseling was taking eighteen hours a week, an impossible burden for a pastor in charge of a local church. In desperation I tried bringing counselees with similar needs together in a group. I was the leader, and we used study books as our common center of attention. The outside reading became the springboard for a more personal sharing. The same relationships of mutual trust-building seemed as possible in the group as they had been in the one-to-one relationship. Immediately my counseling load was cut considerably, though the more disturbed persons still required personal, supportive hours.

While my several therapy groups were meeting (during the late fifties), the idea of a "parish plan" began to receive elaborate promotion. It *sounded* great—having the congregation divided into neighborhoods and meeting in small groups in the homes. Think of the trust and spiritual growth—and programs—that could be built through such a structure!

My enthusiasm ebbed, however, in the face of three overwhelming problems. One was the time required for record keeping on our highly mobile congregation. Second, members with the skill, or will, to host such groups were at a premium, even if we stopped everything else the church was doing. Third, and most important, people in this day simply will not be manipulated into small groups based on something as flimsy as neighborhood boundaries. Moreover, the large majority simply didn't feel the need enough to make the effort.

When denominational papers continued reporting how well the parish plan was working in some larger churches, I decided to see for myself with a hedge-hopping trip across the country. I was stunned! In spite of glowing reports and foolproof paper plans, very little was actually taking place. In a few areas the plan had gotten out of the church office and into the neighborhood, only to deteriorate into a telephone chain for parish promotion, or at best an annual personal visit by the neighborhood leader. The idea was just too broad and artificial to engender an ongoing fellowship where personal growth could actually take place.

I had a painful insight into the ministerial character on that 1959 trip. Time and again, while sitting with a pastor in his study and discussing his church's parish plan efforts, I became inspired. His buoyant outlook tempted me to rush home and put the plan into action in my church. But then, before leaving, I mingled with others on the church staff. The assistant in from the field told me how few members were really involved. The secretary told me how impossible the record-keeping task was. The custodian told me what the laymen were really saying about the plan being handed down. Deflated by the harsh realities of an inoperable idea and pastoral blindness, I finally lost interest in the parish plan.

The trip wasn't wasted, though, because I discovered at Christ Methodist Church in Charleston, West Virginia, an exciting small-group plan that worked and a pastor, Truman Potter, who was both aware and sensitive.

The Christ Church congregation had a large number of prayer-study-sharing groups which met every week; some had been meeting consistently for several years. Since many of the people in that town were scientists engaged in research projects, the groups were attractively called "spiritual research groups." I didn't hear about them from the pastor's lips. Instead, I was met at the plane by a layman who took me out for supper and witnessed to me how "the group" had saved him from the brink of suicide, reconstructed his broken marriage, and quickened his mind and soul until the love of God was the supreme reality in his life.

The next morning, after the traditional tour of the church plant, the pastor took me to his study where half a dozen men and women were assembled to tell me how the groups had revolutionized their lives, changed the life of the church, and deeply affected the life of the community. These people had left their jobs and families to come and share their excitement with me, a total stranger. I felt as if I had discovered the gold at the end of the rainbow.

An enthusiastic young businessman, a former leader in the Fellowship of Christian Athletes, drove me to the plane. He hadn't been at the church; his testimony was reserved for a parting shot. He told how the group was a way of life for his wife and himself and had made Christ real, even relevant, to his business. He was still sharing as I ran through the gate to catch the plane.

As the aircraft lifted off, I knew that I had found what I had been searching for. I was going home to start spiritual research groups.

The people of Christ Church had introduced me to a text-

13

book they often used to begin their groups, *Two or Three Together* by Harold Freer and Frances Hall. Because it provides a fine beginning for the prayer-sharing-study type of small group, each person or couple in the three groups we now started purchased a copy.

The plan was simple. We agreed to a mutual discipline of regular attendance for ten weeks, at which time we would evaluate whether or not to continue. We prayed for each other by name every day and studied the assigned chapter. When we came together each week at the church, we entered and sat in silence for thirty minutes, all meditating on the same material from the text. The members took turns being timekeepers. At the end of thirty minutes of private meditation, we began an equal time of sharing.

The silence always accomplished something amazing. There was a togetherness, a depth of common concern which allowed us to deal immediately with personal needs. The small talk had been skimmed off, and we were of "one accord" (Acts 1:14). Some groups decided to break up after the original ten weeks, but others stayed together several years. After the original thirty meditations in Freer and Hall's book, we alternated between one of the books of the New Testament and some devotional classic like Thomas Kelly's *A Testament of Devotion*.

I also began to use this approach in my groups of counselees. For both groups—those who were disturbed enough to come for counseling and the laymen who voluntarily sought out a group—the personal relationship involved sustained them through many times of crisis and frequently opened the door to a personal relationship with Christ.

I began to suspect that it wasn't the content of the material which we read that was important; primarily, the material served as a springboard to personal relationships. *It had not yet dawned on me that the material we studied often became a block to genuine personal growth.* Why? Because some in the groups found it easy to deal only at a theoretical level with ideas and never really center on the need of a person to change his attitude or behavior.

In 1963 I moved from Phoenix, Arizona, to a new congregation in Long Beach, California. By this time variations on the "group" theme were sweeping the country, though that should not imply a mass acceptance of the movement. In fact, only a small number of pastors seemed willing to practice what their professional journals were preaching. The thought of small groups meeting apart from their control seemed to threaten many ministers. The thought of being in a group was even more threatening.

I have come to see that this phenomenon is all tied up with the minister's self-image. Apparently I was too naive then to recognize the threat. When it came, I had to ride it through. I shall refer later to the traumatic experiences yet in store for me when the group got off books and into the area of openness about feelings.

My predecessor had conducted a prayer therapy group, which was still meeting. The group used Dr. William Parker's book *Prayer Can Change Your Life*, which pursues a psychologically based program of testing, group sharing, and prayer aimed at honesty about feelings and self-understanding. The process brought a new openness to God, which in turn brought healing as the power of God's love came in. The group had clearly saved the lives of several disturbed persons and enabled them to come through to creative living.

I did not feel competent to lead the group. The program of psychological testing was not within my training, and I observed that the group tended to become bogged down in psychological analysis rather than discovering new freedom in personal communication. I encouraged them to continue meeting, and they did so as a prayer-sharing-study group with the emphasis on intercessory prayer. (Some of the experiences related in Dr. Parker's book are forerunners of what we now call the encounter group.)

15

We tried other group experiments which combined study, sharing, prayer, and service. Cottage prayer meetings on a neighborhood basis were conducted for special seasons. Other groups that were committed to some specific project, like visitation envangelism, were called "The Twelve." Twelve persons committed themselves to a common discipline: meeting weekly for study and prayer and, on the fourth week, working on their service project.

I am confident that therapy and spiritual growth take place whenever Christians get together in sustained and sustaining relationships. However, the persons participating in these groups always seemed to be "the same old crowd," who always showed up whenever there was a "church program." As with the parish plan, these groups and projects were superimposed on the congregation and required all the promotion that is usually associated with such programs. Furthermore, it was all too easy for persons to remain superficial, hiding behind intellectual discussions and presuming that attendance in itself was virtuous.

One of the first things I did upon coming to the new congregation was to begin a spiritual research group. Into that group came a number of persons from the prayer therapy experiment, bringing with them a refreshing depth of honesty then unfamiliar to me. Determined to be open also, I sought personal strength from the group. One night one of the members, our organist, said, "You know, Stan, for the first time you don't act like you're in control of the situation." Though she was right, her freedom to say how she felt made me uncomfortable. Yet I was grateful and excited because she helped me see how I was coming across to others, and how they felt about me. The experience was a portent of greater things to come.

Into that particular group came a young businessman who was working his way through college, going to night classes. He had felt God calling him to the pastoral ministry. His name was Bob Deits, and how he got there is the subject of the next chapter.

Chapter 2

□

Called to Be
(The Encounter)

BOB DEITS:

My first meeting with a spiritual research group was one of those experiences that I only later recognized as a crossroads event in my life. The evening was pleasant, the spiritual research format different from the prayer therapy style I was used to, and I was glad to get better acquainted with our new pastor, Stan Brown. But it was hardly an earthshaking experience. My wife, June, and I did not lie awake all night pondering its significance. Besides, the earthshaking had already taken place for us some years earlier. The mere fact that we were participating in a small group in a church must have registered a solid seven on the heavenly Richter scale.

For June and me, church was not a part of our childhood or teenage years. We had that much in common when we married a few months after graduating from high school. It's amazing how little you know of another person at eighteen, even after five years of going together. It's also amazing how much you *think* you know! I have concluded that both of these phenomena result from knowing so terribly little about yourself. No wonder the mortality rate on teenage marriages is so high!

We married at eighteen—became parents at nineteen and again at twenty-one—and were ready for divorce at twenty-three. Five years of tension, frustration, and all-night arguments had taken a heavy toll on our idealistic images of marriage. Communication seemed impossible. Worries about money, tension over sex, June's fear of pregnancy, my poor showing at work—all these things made our lives a nightmare. In a futile effort to find peace, I drank more and more.

Outwardly, June and I put on a good show. We were the "party kids" who liked a good time—that "nice young couple with those cute little boys." Inwardly, so far in that we scarcely mentioned it to ourselves, we were dying to each other.

In desperation and almost without realizing why, June turned to the church. A neighbor who attended Grace Methodist Church near our home in Long Beach, California, invited June to go to church with her. Wanting no part of religion, I stayed home. The following week was especially rough between us, and one day June sat down before the telephone with tears in her eyes and a lawyer's business card in her hand. At that exact moment, the church's pastor came calling.

The Reverend Dwight Bennett was one of those men whose eyes see beneath the skin and whose ears hear the heart as well as the voice. Only years later did we learn how much he had "read" in one brief meeting with June. We're just glad that it was enough to send him out to see what was going on in our household. His visit did more than interrupt a telephone call; it gave June hope. She filed away the attorney's card (we never have found that card!) and began convincing me that I should go to church with her.

I liked Dwight Bennett. I didn't really want to, but I did. He didn't preach; he listened. He didn't tell us to stop being sinful; he invited us to come with him to an Ashram in the high Sierras. He became our friend. Instead of giving us rules, he gave us a relationship. Six months after his visit, on the basis of that relationship, we went with him to the Ashram. It was August, 1957.

(Dr. E. Stanley Jones, the missionary, evangelist, and author, brought the Ashram movement to America from India. The word means "a retreat." The format is a disciplined corporate quest for deeper spiritual growth that will make God more real in daily living. For more information write: United Christian Ashrams, W. W. Richardson, General Secretary, 60 Bluff Road, Barrington, Rhode Island 02860.)

The strange surroundings and activities of a Christian camp were terrifying, but Dwight Bennett was always there, and so was a layman from the same church. They encouraged, chided, and listened—always they listened—to the outpourings of a shaken young couple.

There, too, was Dr. E. Stanley Jones, who showed us the hope of a whole new life. One afternoon June and I knelt with him in a rustic old cabin and uttered the first prayers of our adult life. In the traditional parlance of the church, it was a conversion experience. Whatever you call it, a new thing happened to us through those men. I began to hear my wife. She began to hear me. Jesus Christ and his church became the foundation for a new relationship.

After eighteen months, however, we had to admit that "being Christian" had not enabled us to grow sufficiently as persons. We went to church, prayed, and read the Bible, but it wasn't enough. Wholeness as persons was still in front of us somewhere. A baby daughter didn't bring it, and my decision to study for the ministry only heightened the desire for it.

This decision was reached a year after our first Ashram experience. One day, I went to work as usual. As I walked into my office, I suddenly knew I was going into the ministry. It was that fast and that simple. Until the moment it happened, the thought had not consciously crossed my mind. Two weeks later, I was enrolled in night classes at Long Beach City College.

At Dwight Bennett's suggestion, my wife and I formed a

small group. At virtually the same time that Stan Brown was traveling across the country searching for ways to bring new life to people, ten persons searching for wholeness began meeting every Friday evening in our home. The group adopted a prayer-and-share format. We spent the first few minutes meditating on a common Bible passage, then shared with each other exactly what was happening in our lives, good and bad. Almost at once, we discovered that sharing was the most important part of our group meeting. None of us were trained in psychology or familiar with "encounter" and "sensitivity training." Nevertheless, our experience taught us that openness and honesty were keys to a meaningful group experience.

At first, it was excruciating for June and me to talk out our personal problems in front of eight other people, including our pastor. What would they think? How could I admit that I was afraid of people and then expect these same folks to support me as a candidate for the ministry? What if I said that my shyness made me a poor husband and a lousy lover? Yet, in time, everything that bothered me came out in the open. In fact, the more honest I was, the more acceptance I experienced from the group. I learned that other people had the same fears I did. Even the pastor, Dwight Bennett, understood what was going on inside me.

The group became a new "family" for us. Friday evening was the focal point of the week; Sunday worship was an act of celebration in the truest sense. Just to meet a fellow group member on the street was to experience instant affirmation.

For June and me the same candid-yet-loving relationship of the group became the basis of our marriage relationship. We found a whole new freedom of expression and acceptance of each other, with no pretenses. Our problems did not simply melt away, of course, but we did begin to deal with them. Most important, perhaps, was finding love and acceptance in each other as we were—*without change*.

It is significant that my sales volume increased markedly

and I moved into a junior executive position. The explanation is simple. As I learned to trust the group, my fears of other people began to diminish. If the people who knew everything about me accepted and loved me, why should I fear the rest of the world?

For more than three years, we met every Friday evening, and the miracle of new birth was forever present. The group grew to nearly twenty persons, too many for such intimate sharing. Yet, most of those who participated were radically affected by the experience. Today a special bond of fellowship still unites those who shared in it.

The popularity and effectiveness of that group led to the formation of a prayer therapy group in the style created by Dr. William Parker of the University of Redlands. It brought to us participants a deeper psychological insight into ourselves and further underscored to me the need for a high degree of openness in group relationships.

On the basis of these small group experiences and their life-shaping impact upon my marriage, I determined that if I made it to ordination, groups would play a major role in my ministry. Through the groups, Christian faith had reached deep into my life at the places where I really lived. I wanted faith to make a difference at those places or not at all.

In 1963 Stan Brown became the pastor of Grace Methodist Church in Long Beach. I was delighted to discover his interest in small groups in the church. When he introduced the spiritual research group described in chapter 1, June and I eagerly agreed to participate. What a joy to establish an authentic relationship with another pastor who was a real person! What none of us realized was that the Lord had something more in mind.

A year later the long-awaited day came when I finished college, resigned my job, and enrolled in the School of Theology at Claremont, California. My first ministerial assignment was to the First Methodist Church of Montebello, near

Los Angeles. I was to be the youth minister—a task about which I knew absolutely nothing!

Soon, however, a small group of college students was meeting weekly in our home. Over a period of six months that group (1) prevented a suicide attempt by a girl, (2) reunited an eighteen-year-old boy with his family, (3) brought three persons into the church, and (4) resulted in the marriage of two members. I was now convinced that small groups belonged at the center of the church's youth ministry.

An investigation of other churches uncovered much interest, some talk, but few programs of this type. So many of the activities planned by adult counselors for the youth seemed to be just that: adult ideas imposed upon tolerating youth. The youth groups I had missed as a teenager seemed at best to have left in my contemporaries a few fond memories—cabin raids and volleyball games followed by a short prayer with the "thees" and "thous" all mixed up. Was that all there was? I thought of the girl who, at nineteen, was ready to take her life—there *had* to be a way to hear such cries for help. Now I've learned that the best thing any adult counselor has to offer a young person is an honest and understanding relationship. Nothing else really matters.

In theology school, my interest in groups was further stimulated by Dr. Howard J. Clinebell. In his class lectures and books (*Mental Health Through Christian Community* and *Basic Types of Pastoral Counseling*) he stressed the need to build emotional strength as well as spiritual strength in people. He gave me a new grasp of the changes in my life and new insight into my hang-ups.

A program sponsored by the Lilly Foundation permitted me to participate with other seminary students in a small group led by Dr. Clinebell. In it being phony became a near impossibility. Whatever vestige of a "ministerial image" I still had was rapidly dissolved.

When I looked around me and looked into a mirror, I despaired for the future of the church. What neurotics we were! Then it slowly dawned on me that we in that group represented a good average slice of American Protestant church life. No better. No worse. The only difference was that we had turned honest.

I wondered what would happen if a minister carried that same transparency into his church. Remembering that it was Dwight Bennett's openness, not his righteousness, that attracted me, I went to the church and shared my story with the congregation. The response was immediate and gratifying. The church members seemed overjoyed to know that a preacher was alive to the same struggles they were facing. What a relief for me! No more pious "ministerial image." I could be myself.

During our two years at the Montebello Methodist Church, June and I maintained contact with the Browns and our relationship developed into a deep friendship. We shared continually as our involvement in groups deepened. The real meaning of that first spiritual research group became clear when the Lord ordained (with help from the bishop) that I should return to Grace Methodist Church to work as associate pastor with Stan Brown.

As he and I began to design a strategy for ministry in the church, groups were central in our thinking. But what kinds of groups? What role should groups play in the total ministry of the church? When the Conference youth ministry director offered a training event for youth ministers, I attended, expecting only to gather some new "how-to" knowledge. To my surprise, we were divided into small groups and were put through what has come to be called "sensitivity training." I was excited because here was a way to stimulate authentic relationships between people in a short period of time. This process offered the tools for enabling a person to do the kind of hearing that had been so valuable in my life. I was eager to try it with our young people.

A short time later Stan and I successfully introduced the process at a weekend youth retreat. The young people responded overwhelmingly with acceptance and love for each other. Furthermore, even though we had spent almost no time "being religious," thirty-eight out of forty young people went to the altar to make a new commitment to Jesus Christ! For some, the experience was a life-changing factor.

The last link in the chain defining our ministry together was added by Stan Brown when he took the same process to a small group of young married couples. Again, the results indicated that such "encounter" experiences were a vital, life-changing force in the church.

We began to think about further extensions of the encounter principle. What did it mean to our total ministry? Would it work in staff meetings and planning sessions? What about church school? The possibilities were endless—and a little frightening. We were grateful to the Lord for bringing us to this point, and we believed that he was opening a new door for us. But before we could consider the risks of such a step, we had to know if encounter groups were legitimately within the framework of our biblical faith.

Chapter 3

□

Called to Follow
(The Plan)

STAN and BOB:

Five young men are planning to infiltrate a town and capture it for Jesus Christ. Sound revolutionary? It is!

In college these young men banded together in answer to Christ's call for total commitment to the fulfillment of his kingdom. They believe this to be the most radical claim leading to the most revolutionary way of life the world has ever known.

To prepare themselves, they decided to devote their summers to working with E. Stanley Jones, studying the Bible with him, and soaking up everything he would say on the Ashram circuit. When they have learned all they can, they will settle and seek employment in a city of about 35,000 people and attempt to multiply their commitment until the whole town is living for God.

Around the world today are groups of Christ-centered persons who are preparing themselves and others by banding together in small groups, learning all they can from each other, and moving out to repeat the process in relationship to others. This is basically the plan Jesus used. Let's see how he developed this plan.

Most Christians now realize that to be the church is to be in mission, recreating the body of Christ in the world where we live. For some congregations, unfortunately, this has meant jumping into water over their heads without adequate training in how to swim. Too many preachers are telling their people to do something for which they are unprepared and uncommitted. Jesus knew this danger and never sent his disciples out to do something for which they were not prepared.

He also shared the dilemma of modern man: how to minister to a whole society when meeting one individual's needs can take so much time. Yet he continually sought new people to love and to serve. When the elders of the town of Capernaum urged him to settle down and be their physician, he said to his men, *Let us go on to the next towns, that I may preach there also; for that is why I came out* (Mark 1: 38). After he came to one of those "next towns," he was met by a pleading leper and *moved with pity, he stretched out his hand and touched him . . .* Mark 1:41).

The word "pity" (or "compassion") is repeated eight times in the gospels, referring to Jesus' feeling for the people. Most of us have had a similar emotion while standing on a hill or in a tall building at night and looking out over the lights of the community. Suddenly we remember that those lights represent people. *When he saw the crowds, he had compassion for them, because they were harassed and helpless, like sheep without a shepherd* (Matthew 9:36).

Compassion is the strongest word in the Greek to describe the feeling of concern and love that moves up from the core of a person's being. It is the ability to feel with another and put that feeling into loving action. This was the holy restlessness which drove the Master from one needy person to another, from one hungry family to another, from one spiritually destitute town to another. It is one of the basic sensitivities a follower of Jesus must have, haunting him with a sense of unfinished mission.

Because the Lord never saw his public ministry as a "one-man operation," he called men and women to follow him. Joining the band of followers were persons from all walks of life. Some of John the Baptist's disciples spent a night with Jesus around a campfire in the Judean wilderness and decided to follow him. They went and got their friends. Jesus spent a fruitful hour with a Samaritan woman by Jacob's well, and she ran to invite the whole town to meet him. He shared the cool of an evening with Nicodemus and gave him the vision of new birth. He accepted the hospitality of Zacchaeus in Jericho, the two sisters and Lazarus in Bethany, the mother of John Mark in Jerusalem, Peter's family in Capernaum, bringing with him a new way of life they experienced as love, joy, peace, patience, kindness, goodness, faithfulness, gentleness, and self control (Galatians 5:22, 23a).

As the months passed, his followers increased. Some came along only for the day, others for weeks or months. Jesus identified himself with the people: preaching to them, healing their sick, gathering their children, giving himself so that at times he could not even get away to eat.

Unfortunately, the crowds insisted on misinterpreting his message. They eagerly took his food and accepted his healing, but they did not understand his talk about the kingdom of God and the need for a revolutionary loyalty. Revolution meant only one thing to them: the overthrow of Rome and a return to the theocracy of David's time. Zealots with swords up their sleeves and peasants overwhelmed by poverty wanted to identify Jesus as the military messiah who would lead them to establish an earthly kingdom.

Later, perhaps in the second year of his ministry, our Lord changed his strategy. He chose twelve men to be a close circle of disciples, and eventually he chose an even more select group of three from the twelve. Mark's description of their appointment catches the importance of this plan: *And he appointed twelve, to be with him, and to be sent out to preach and have authority to cast out demons* (Mark 3:14—

15). In the drama of preaching and healing we too easily overlook the element which came first: *to be with him.*

A masterful program now begins to unfold. Jesus spent more and more of his time with the disciples and less with the crowds. The group made retreats into the mountains and visited the surrounding provinces. This pattern became increasingly evident, as recorded in John 11:54—*Jesus therefore no longer went about openly among the Jews, but went from there to the country near the wilderness. . .and there he stayed with the disciples.*

Jesus did not reject the crowds, however, for when they came seeking him, he was available. For the disciples, every day brought a new learning experience. When Jesus ministered to others, it was a class for the disciples, who were always close at hand. After telling the crowd a parable in a few minutes, Jesus could spend an hour explaining its meaning in dialogue with the disciples. They ate and slept, walked and sailed, fished and worked together day after day. In fact, this closeness with Jesus was the way the disciples were identified. A maid from the house of the high priest recognized Peter because, as she said, *You also were with the Nazarene, Jesus* (Mark 14:67).

The secret of his method was not in his teaching, but in *who he was in relationship to the members of this intimate group.* For example, he prayed and referred to the Father as the source of his power so often that the disciples asked him to teach them to pray. Whereas we might have been tempted to lecture about the subject, Jesus placed on their lips an actual prayer.

They shared with him in the synagogue worship, in the retreats, in the soul-searching struggles with others who sought some light. They were beside him in the great confrontations with officials of the establishment, and in meeting the physical needs of common folk. He sent them out on short missions to try it for themselves (Luke 9, 10). When they failed, he was there to pick up the pieces (Luke 9:39—

43); when they succeeded, he celebrated with them (Luke 10: 17–24).

Again and again we find the group having the freedom to be open about their feelings, showing a high level of trust. Jesus could discuss who they thought he was, how they pleased or displeased him, how much he loved them, and how they frustrated him by their slowness to believe. The followers were free to admit their ignorance and feelings of inadequacy, to boast feelings of trust and loyalty, and even to reveal angry emotions. These frequent exchanges at the feeling level show the real growth of trust and understanding between the disciples and Jesus.

This group stayed together in a growing intimacy, apparently for three years. Note that there were women as well as men in the close followers—women who came from both the higher social strata and the lower edges of social acceptance. Yet there is not one scrap of evidence to indicate a scandal. These men and women traveled together up and down the land, camping out or using each other's homes, but no one pointed a finger to accuse them of indecency. Surely if there had been a thread of gossip, it would have crystalized in the charges trumped up against Jesus at his trials or in the efforts to discredit him after the resurrection, but there is nothing of the sort. It seems fair to say that Christian encounter groups today can be loving and intimate and achieve high levels of trust without being subject to the immoral suggestions of impure minds.

Certainly the disciples had all the feelings of lust, ambition, jealousy, and greed that plague the rest of us. They showed these feelings, sometimes succumbed to them, but the power of acceptance and trust in their group lifted them to higher levels. It so prepared them that they were receptive to the "power from on high" and became capable of going out to repeat the process with others.

The disciples and followers of Christ probably were too caught up in the exciting experiences of the moment to see the unfolding of a plan that would turn the world upside down. Jesus compared it to a mustard seed that begins so small but grows so large. The world would reject him, as it would each of the others in turn, but it could not defeat the cause or destroy those committed to it. These people discovered their freedom to be vulnerable, since they lived not to court popularity but to glorify and enjoy the kingdom of God. No one can beat that!

Tragically, the modern church has missed this strategy. We talk about evangelism and Christian nurture, but take so little time for close, personal encounter. We invite people to the church, give them a few classes, and leave them on their own. Too often they lose the glow and fall by the side.

Formerly, when instructing visitation teams, we pointed to the parable of the sower, the point being that only 25 percent of the seed fell on good ground and took root. And, sure enough, we could count on that same percentage of calls to bear fruit in terms of church members. But when many of these members later became "dead wood," we should have asked ourselves "Why?"—particularly since Jesus lost only one out of the twelve.

Like the Master, we are, first, to present the good news to everyone who will listen, and, second, to minister to all comers. Following his example, we take those who are ready and concentrate on going deeper with them until we are all disciples who know the truth that makes us free. Jesus' intimacy with the twelve shows us that the church is meant to be more than just another community organization, more than a house of worship. It is a fellowship of believers gathered around the Spirit of Christ and engaged in the slow, painstaking work of making disciples.

At the end of the first gospel stands the Lord's great commission: *All authority in heaven and on earth has been given to me. Go therefore and make disciples of all nations, baptizing them in the name of the Father and of the Son and of the Holy Spirit, teaching them to observe all that I have commanded you; and lo, I am with you always, to the close of the age* (Matthew 28:18–20).

For some reason we have interpreted this in terms of a sweeping global mission. Perhaps such phrases as "all nations" have obscured the basic commission, which is to "make disciples." The New English Bible translation, "make all nations *my* disciples," clearly implies that discipleship should not be formed around anything less than Jesus Christ.

Does all of this mean that the local pastor should take a few of his congregation who are ready to go deeper and spend an increasing portion of his time with them in the development of discipleship? This book is the record of two pastors who decided to try it.

To follow the Master's plan required a reordering of our use of time, new attitudes toward our role and self-image, and a new psychological contract with our people. The next section shares the agony of developing a new style of ministry and what happened to us and our congregations when we did.

PART TWO

"God Chose What Is Weak"

. . . but God chose what is foolish in the world to shame the wise, God chose what is weak in the world to shame the strong, God chose what is low and despised in the world, even things that are not, to bring to nothing things that are, so that no human being might boast in the presence of God. (I Corinthians 1:27-29)

Chapter 4

□

Folly or Power

STAN:

New discoveries call for new actions. Nowhere is this more true than in the discovery of Jesus of Nazareth. When men and women encountered him in Palestine, they felt compelled to make radical changes in their life-styles. So do people today. My life as a Christian is a continuing encounter with Jesus Christ, now here, now there. His meaning in my life deepens as the years go by.

When I discovered his plan of taking a few persons and going deeper with them in personal growth and encounter, I faced an awesome decision. I could either ignore the implications and continue running the church like a top executive in a multifaceted corporation, or I could center on teaching and personal relationships, cutting the corporation loose to run itself. Three issues were at stake: (1) my use of time; (2) my role as an authority figure; and (3) my definition of ministry.

The last thing I wanted to do was to put in more time. My workdays often ran to fourteen hours; sometimes weeks went by without a day off and with only a few hours chiseled out for my wife and children. I was trapped in an impossible schedule and felt too guilty to break out of it—an all-too-common pastoral hang-up. It began to dawn on me that if I were more honest about my real importance and more free to follow my conscience, I would spend less time at the church and more time with my family. In any case, I could not add more "groups" to everything I was already doing. If I took our Lord's priorities seriously, I needed to change my whole use of time and to reevaluate my values.

A painful question arose: How much of my struggle was really over the use of time, and how much of it was over the release of my authority as a "high-powered executive"? I have since heard other pastors tell how they cannot give time to small groups because they are too busy with important meetings or social action projects. That style is certainly theirs to choose, but my temptation was to hide behind these things in order to save my authoritarian image.

It was really depressing to find that my ego was so heavily invested in time-consuming activities outside my local church. I was a committee chairman and member of the executive committee of both our area Council of Churches and our denominational Conference Board of Evangelism. At one point I was president of the city ministerial association, which made an an ex-officio member of the Armed Services, YMCA Board, and a trustee of a large hospital. There were uncounted meals, meetings, trips, secretarial efforts, telephone calls, and, of course, friendships with the important people of the community and the denomination. I enjoyed being known and acknowledged by name in these circles. Who wants to give that up just to stay home and lead a few groups?

Another issue intruded into my consciousness: Had I been traveling a road that did not lead to the goal of my ministry? Let me see, that goal is to enable people to enter the kingdom of God. Did I have the title of a minister of Christ when, in fact, many of my activities did not bring persons any closer to him? I became increasingly convinced that the kingdom of God does not thrive on programs, statistics, and public relations, but exists in personal relationships. Programs and action projects can lead to relationships, but in my experience they were doing little to free people or enable them to experience God's love. *If my ministry meant majoring in personal relationships, then the programs and committees had to go.* Others might have a different answer. For me, there was no alternative.

Yet I was sometimes embarrassed by my decision. For example, I had chaired a committee that rewrote the constitution of our local Council of Churches, instituting a flexible task force approach instead of standing committees. One task force was on "witness," an activity that I had long complained was conspicuous by its absence from our cooperative efforts. After the revised constitution was adopted, the council asked me to chair the task force on witness. I felt obligated to accept, but eventually phased myself out of the responsibility because the meetings conflicted with my encounter group sessions.

My denominational responsibilities also pressured me. I felt I was failing the leadership invested in me for committees and projects, yet these activities didn't seem to be leading to the fulfillment of my goal. I was haunted by the belief that the denominational and ecumenical machinery was perpetuating a mutual backscratching operation and little more, while in the groups and the preaching services lives were being changed and sustained. On the other hand, there must be more to all the organizational machinery than I could see because so many men and women whom I respected were devoting time and energy to these structures.

If loyalty to the kingdom of God transcends denomination, community, and even nation, then I *had* to eliminate this conflict. I made a very personal decision—to resign my committees and chairmanships. This was the only *right* action for *me.* At last I could come to grips with the problems of my use of time, my role of authority, and my definition of ministry. These pastoral demons had to be dealt with more than once, but at least they were now identified.

Next came the task of educating my congregation for my new role. The pastor is ever dependent on the good will of his people, even in a connectional system like mine. It is important to know and meet their expectations, and the congregations I have known have expected their pastor to be a professional "comforter-promoter-saint." A super-Christian!

Comfort is expected for needs great and small, and the pastor soon learns whose needs are most demanding.

He is allowed to promote his own and the denomination's programs if he can balance them comfortably. Everyone knows he is expected to produce certain statistical and visual results as he maneuvers his committees and laity—so the congregation permits him to "do his thing" even when they must smile indulgently and not knowingly.

In the role of "saint," the pastor is allowed by his people to sound the note of judgment, again in the line of duty, as long as he remains on his pedestal. His freedom to speak the truth is in exchange for the knowledge that at least someone lives up to it. The pastor-saint must be a holy man who does not bring the ugly world too close as he goes about trailing the incense of his sacramental functions.

If I was to be an enabler of personal growth, if the real needs of people were to become my pastoral priority, then the old roles of comforter, promoter, and saint had to be redefined. In a later chapter I will share what happened to my "sainthood." As a "comforter," always present to hold the hands of shut-ins and committee chairmen, my circuit-riding days were numbered. I could not possibly attend all the meetings, make all the calls, or grant all the favors expected of me. The criteria for attention had to be the real need of the person, member or not.

Of course, I called on persons who were really sick or in trouble or waging personal struggles. But I also began to emphasize the need for training members of the congregation to share this mission. Teaching church members that every Christian is a minister and has a pastoral function is not easy. These people have come to be ministered to, and often their faithfulness is based on "what they get out of the service."

To retool the congregation, I began preaching often on the church as the body of Christ in the world, and that if there was any mission, we all shared it together. Several weekly prayer groups began praying for the Holy Spirit to be poured out on the congregation, filling us all with the compassion and power of God.

The worship services became more informal, with time for personal greeting and increasing participation by the congregation. This participation did not center in liturgy but in more personal involvement, such as individual sharing in spoken prayers and various one-to-one encounter techniques. (For example, everyone writes down the uppermost concern of his heart; the slips are collected and distributed, and the concern that a person receives becomes his prayer for the week ahead. Or, the pastor goes down the aisle, holds both hands of each person at the end of the pew, looks into his eyes, and says, "God loves you and I love you." Each person turns and says this to his neighbor, passing the greeting down the row.) These approaches are specifically designed to enable the congregation to become a caring fellowship. Furthermore, visitation groups carried the vital personal touch to shut-ins, prospective members, and delinquent members.

As an abdicating "promoter," I had to enable the laymen to initiate and carry out the church's programs, a task more difficult to teach than pastoral care. Most established congregations are schooled in the belief that if you sit in a committee meeting and restate the problem, something has been accomplished. The committee member goes home with the good feeling that he has done something for God and can now dismiss the whole affair until the next meeting, when the problems are again rehearsed. This is an overstatement for emphasis, but sadly true at its core. To fight this mentality, we began a changeover from commissions, committees, and boards to a freer style of work areas. We elected chairmen, who recruited task leaders, who did specific jobs.

The involvement of laymen in the mission and ministry of the church required a new approach by our church staff. Every church has a staff, no matter how small the congregation. Our staff meetings always included the custodian, the nursery coordinator, the secretaries, the organist, the choir director(s), some regular office volunteers, the associate pastor, and the pastor. Together we thought of ourselves as a team, all ministers in our respective tasks. We met weekly and spent time in Bible study, sharing, and prayer. We used to look over the church program, decide what needed to be done, and assign responsibility for the tasks among the staff. I would take these decisions to our elected officials (if I remembered to), tell them what was already decided, and expect them to rubber-stamp our plans.

However, my function as trainer and enabler meant a switch in tactics. The creating and carrying out of the church's program must come from the laymen. Their mission: to accomplish Christ's mission, not to be "yes men" for the pastor. Consequently, a small fellowship of officers and work area chairmen replaced the large board (except for required occasional business such as budgets and elections).

This smaller group began meeting monthly to initiate and administer the program. I was member (but not chairman) of this program council, and the multitude of materials that streamed across my desk was immediately distributed to the proper work area chairman, usually by way of his mail box in the church office.

Working in concert, these laymen learned to determine the priorities of our mission and to develop the strategy for carrying them out. I was one of the planners, and a resource person, but I did not take the primary responsibility for executing plans. Making this changeover in emphasis and function in my long-established congregation took several years and much leadership effort. Easing out of the old stereotypes was often tedious and discouraging.

In the present structure of most congregations, the buck stops at the desk of the pastor-in-charge. That is why the temptation to turn back from enabler to promoter was especially strong in my relationship to the other staff members. Was I willing to trust others to carry out their ministry in their own unique way, or did I have to make sure they did it my way? Was I willing to let them fail (and thereby learn and grow), or did I feel compelled to step in and make sure everything was a success? Was I willing to live within a truly shared ministry? Was I willing to be an arm of the body, or must I be the head? Could I actually trust Christ to be the head and, in turn, trust the other members of the staff and the congregation to be obedient to him without constant reference to me?

If I answered yes, this meant that, once we had agreed on areas of ministry, each staff member and lay worker would be free to make decisions and put them into action without having to check everything out with the "head man." Yes meant I would share the failures as well as the victories of these fellow workers. Yes meant we would be a fellowship of peers—laymen and pastors—learning to love and trust one another. To this end we must spend time with one another, not just in church business but in prayer, study, personal sharing, and fun times as well.

Early in this reevaluation of my ministry, I made a sad discovery: The people I spent the most time with in our church were the people with whom I had very little spiritual fellowship. As a pastor I prayed and discussed theology with countless strangers and casual friends, but whenever I was with the officers of the church, we only talked business. I had a deep hunger to be ministered to by these laymen, a desire that together we search out the kingdom along with our programs.

At my request the officers of the program council (policy

committee, council on ministries, etc.) began meeting weekly. We prayed together orally, we sat in creative silences together, we spent long periods considering the purpose of the church and the nature of the kingdom. Within a few months I was encouraged by our new harmony. Though many of us in this leadership group had different opinions on matters that might once have split us into factions, we were learning how to be a family. We were learning to be honest about our feelings, to listen to each other, to subordinate our personal desires to the needs of the others, and to remind each other of our mutual cause.

After that when a controversial issue came up, the officers and pastor were in communication from the beginning. We understood what wrestlings with conscience each was going through, and in the atmosphere of prayer and openness to the Holy Spirit, the issues were dealt with "in love preferring one another."

Since we were honest and in close communication, factions could hardly form unless a person overtly sought to be divisive. Gossip was usually squelched because of ready access to the facts. At meetings, differences of opinion could be openly expressed and close votes taken in a healthy spirit of friendship. Even in the heat of debate, pastor and laymen sensed a warmth of love. Hours in prayer produced a sparkle that said more than the world would ever know about hearts that had opened and souls that were bound together in a common commitment to Christ.

All of these struggles, reevaluations, and changes in style of ministry were precipitated by our decision to follow the Master's plan for his disciples. Now we were ready to plunge in.

BOB:

The implications of an encounter style of ministry reach beyond the pastor-layman relationship; they also have a direct influence on the pastor-pastor relationship. This becomes clear when two or more pastors work on the same staff. When I joined Stan Brown as his associate minister, a well-meaning mutual friend, a layman, said, "Bob, you and Stan are making a big mistake. Your friendship will be destroyed within six months!" I was shocked—not at what he said, but at the awareness of a layman that ministers often have such a difficult time establishing a satisfactory relationship with each other.

On the surface, such a situation seems incongruous with the vocation. Why should two "professional Christians," highly trained in human relations and well-schooled in biblical wisdom about brotherhood, have a serious problem in getting along with each other? It's a good question. One good answer, of course, is that whatever else they are, clergymen are human beings with all the human frailties of anyone else. That in itself guarantees a few problems!

Another answer has to do with the nature of the ministerial role. A minister is expected to be a model of decorum; he mustn't ever "blow his cool." Too, much of what a minister does is vulnerable to second-guessing, especially by his peers. That is, his work is almost totally carried out in interaction with other people. Often a minister is working in a crisis or stress situation where he must make decisions quickly and under pressure. It is seldom clear what action by the minister will be the most fulfilling or enabling to a person or group of persons in a given situation.

Whether his work is "successful" or not is usually known only from the vantage point of a considerable lapse of time. Therefore, the judgmental trap of "I wouldn't have done it that way" looms very large in the relationship between ministers. Add to that the ego-involvement of the job, plus the almost inherent authority-figure problems, and conflict between ministers suddenly seems inevitable instead of impossible.

However, conflict is not inevitable. In spite of these

"occupational hazards," ministers can—and many do—share in a deep and meaningful relationship. The magic ingredient, if there is one, is the same as for anyone else—*investing enough trust in each other to be honest and open*. The only difference is that the level of interaction is so much deeper than in many other situations, and therefore the risk is greater.

Two pastors working closely with each other will reveal a great deal of their personalities, whether willingly or unwillingly. It is simply impossible to share such tasks as preaching, administration, visitation, and counseling and not uncover oneself. To some, this is quite threatening, and as a defense they maintain a reserved "professional" relationship with their coworkers.

Incidentally, another factor crucial to the development of real trust is the establishment (and acceptance) of an order of authority between ministers. As the associate pastor, I was keenly aware of the trust Stan invested in me. I had complete freedom in guiding those areas of our church's mission which were my responsibility. Yet, I knew that any criticism of what I did would ultimately land on him.

We found that there was no such thing as too much communication between us. We spent many hours sharing and formulating ideas, talking over goals, and discussing ways to solve problems. However, the most valuable times were the informal ones. Some of the best programs grew out of our casual chats over coffee at the end of a full Sunday. Such meetings allowed us to encounter each other as persons—not as coworkers, not as senior and associate pastors, not even as friends, but as persons. The result was a deep mutual understanding and acceptance that left no room for conflicts and misunderstandings.

Based on nearly three years of close association with Stan, I am convinced that pastors who have the opportunity to work as a team must also work diligently at their relationship. Those who try to work separately alongside each other are, at best, fools. They are shortchanging their congregations and themselves. They also miss out on a lot of fun! Certainly, in any church considering the use of encounter groups, the pastors must first come to an understanding with each other about their own relationship.

The pastor who serves a church alone has a different problem, as I discovered when I left the staff relationship to become sole pastor of another church. Suddenly, there was no "buddy" with whom to confer, no sharing of dreams, no pooling of ideas. How I longed for someone with whom I could establish the kind of supportive relationship that had become so important to me.

I soon discovered that the answer was not to be found with pastors of neighboring churches. This source should not be ruled out; it just didn't work for me. Conflicting time schedules, divergent needs of the congregations, and subconscious feelings of competition, jealousy, and fear—all these worked against my efforts to relate in depth to fellow pastors.

I decided to try building a solid relationship with a small group of lay people in my church, people with whom a trusting, open, sharing relationship could be established person to person—not *parson* to person! Clearly, such a relationship would depend upon their willingness and mine to bridge the pastor-layman gap.

Into one of two newly formed encounter groups came four young couples, all eager to grow as persons and as Christians. Without any encouragement on my part, they soon let my wife and me know that they wanted to encounter us as persons and not as the parsonage family. If the relationship I was looking for was really possible, it would happen with them. At the time of my transfer to another church, we had been meeting weekly as couples for more than five years.

The spontaneous informal meetings, occasional golf games, and telephone conversations were also important. This group of laymen was crucial to my ongoing personal growth and my effectiveness as a pastor. They helped me keep my personal identity clear and enabled me to "be myself" before the congregation. They, in turn, were a team (not a clique), whether we were celebrating the good news, breaking bread at the Lord's Supper, or sharing in the work of the church.

Admittedly, such a relationship is not always possible between pastor and layman. To attempt it with some persons would be harmful rather than enabling. However, I am convinced that it is possible with a far greater number of persons than the pastor might think. And, more pastors are both open and hungry for such a fellowship than the layman might think.

If openness, authenticity, and loving honesty are to be the marks of a growing church, they must surely characterize the relationship between pastors and between the pastor and some laymen of the church.

Chapter 5

□

Be Foolish in the World

STAN:

No one warned me that so much agony would accompany the ecstasy of making significant discoveries about myself through encounter groups. I just stumbled in, and while my ministry and my life are more joyful and effective now, I am still struggling. I sometimes think wistfully of the days when I moved boldly from one project to another in unbeatable self-confidence, sure that I was the most well-adjusted person I had ever met. So, don't say I didn't warn you.

My first experience in an encounter group was outside the church. A fine hospital in our city of Long Beach, California, had a center for training chaplains and for conducting courses in pastoral counseling and psychotherapy, taught by a professional staff. I enrolled and each week for nine months spent half a day in the counseling center with a large group of pastors. We counseled persons who came to the clinic, reviewed our efforts in seminars, observed experts and each other at work over closed-circuit television, and then spent the last hour and a half in a therapy group. (The class was divided into ongoing groups of about ten each.)

At the outset, I was tempted to cut out and get on to more important things. After all, I said to my wife, I had no problems. I have always considered myself extremely well-balanced, ready to take constructive criticism, sure of my decisions. I was a little disgusted at how many problems some of the other pastors had—hang-ups with children, wives, parishioners, and themselves. I felt especially anxious about the lack of identity as ministers which some of them suffered; on the other hand, some had too strong an identity and came on as pious and authoritarian. Why couldn't they all be stable middle-of-the-roaders like me?

My impatience grew, especially with those who carped about their vocation as ministers. To me, the ministry was the greatest! Anyone with a real calling (like mine) would know that. Their trouble must be a lack of faith or commitment—or probably the absence of a personal relationship with Jesus Christ. I said so.

One day a group member was honest enough to tell me that I was coming through as phony and pious; I always had the final answers, employing a neat turn of a phrase and a summing-up tone of voice. I had a way of dismissing the problems of others as if they were stupid. Now several others dared to chime in. Yes, this was how they felt about me, also.

Who, me? Something is wrong with the way I come across?

When the group broke up a few minutes later, I was wounded and bleeding, my legs were weak, and my mind was reeling. As I slowly drove home, the group's words clashed over and over in my mind. *Can they possibly be right?* I walked into the house like a whipped dog. Fortunately, my wife is a wonderful listener, and lovingly she helped me to realize that maybe I did have some problems after all. Come to think of it, why *was* I always so defensive about my vocation when other ministers complained or occasionally dropped out?

I could hardly wait for the next group meeting so that I could explore and find more of the truth about myself.

I became aware of other people's responses to me. Some members of my congregation had indicated that I was not communicating effectively. How unconsciously I had dismissed the rumblings. Suddenly I began to hear them anew. Secondhand rumors that I was a dictator, that I was not sincere, came to me. That really hurt—no one was more sincere than I! (I identified completely with the "Peanuts" cartoon showing Charlie Brown dragging in off the baseball field and muttering, "I don't understand it! One hundred and thirty-two to nothing! And we were so sincere!")

For the first time in my adult life, I had to face and deal with the fact that no matter how pure I felt I was, I simply wasn't coming across that way. Previously, I had simply rationalized such complaints away. Perhaps I had been in one congregation too long; or, those who didn't like me probably had hang-ups about authority. So much for my parishioners— but here were people *outside the church*, people with whom I had no contract, criticizing me. We owed each other nothing except the freedom to be honest, and these relative strangers were telling me the same things about myself. Obviously, something about the way I communicated to others blocked my effectiveness in sharing the gospel. That made the situation doubly serious. For *my* sake, I might run away from this; for *Christ's* sake, I could not.

A few months after the conclusion of my course at the hospital, I began the first experimental encounter group in our congregation. As my own understanding of this approach grew, so did the number of groups.

My personal growth in spiritual and emotional awareness among my own parishioners continued. Slowly I learned to become a child among them, vulnerable, asking for help. As mutual trust grew, they told me what no one had ever before dared to tell me—things I couldn't have accepted if they had. Let me share some of the exhilarating discoveries of those first two and a half years.

I learned about my *self-confidence*. I had assumed that I

could always do bigger and better things, that there was no limit to my future. My friends in the groups helped me discover that I do have limits in energy, time, and ability; that I cannot do anything and everything, especially single-handedly. I was getting so many irons in the fire and longing to develop so many more programs that my anxiety was showing. Then, when my fortieth birthday rolled around, I began to admit that the horizon was not as endless as I had thought. I could not be author, conference speaker, community leader, preacher, pastor, and statistical wonder and still relate to people in the flesh-and-blood love of Jesus. The group experience helped me to choose and to put some desires aside. I decided that my family should have more of me, and that I wanted to enable others to find their fulfillment instead of thinking all the filling was up to me. A more realistic view of myself gave me the freedom to step out of the center of mission of our church.

In the encounter groups I learned about my sense of *self-importance*. I became aware that people kept apologizing for taking my time. Many who came for counseling or stopped by with a question would say, "I shouldn't take your time. I know you're busy." When this happened, I fervently explained that people were of the greatest importance to me and I had all the time in the world for anyone in need. I said this in sermons and in private conversations, but still the apologies came.

Then, in a group of single adults, we were comparing each other to animals. I turned out to be a chipmunk, a beaver, a ground squirrel. The group was characterizing my busy manner, the furrow in my brow, and the fast pace of my public activities. I saw that in spite of my lip service to having time, I was communicating to people that I was very busy and that it was inconvenient for me to fit them into my busy schedule.

Was I going in so many directions at once that I was never free to be *real*, to be *with* a person unless he was programmed in? I discovered that I should quit taking myself so seriously; instead, I should "hang loose," as it were, and become free to respond to the needs of each moment. But how could I slow down and overcome the air of authority which turned off so many people?

For one thing, I consciously changed my style of preaching from a rapid-fire, come-on-strong delivery to a more conversational tone, using plenty of personal references and not being afraid to share my failures and weaknesses. The results were gratifying both to me and to my congregation.

An unexpected change in my style of dress came about. The members of a new group in which I was participating were making montages to express their self-image. Among the pictures I used was that of a young executive nattily dressed in a business suit. I explained that when I dressed up, I felt confident and self-assured.

Suddenly, as I verbalized this feeling, I recalled the birth of our third child. My wife, Ruth, had gone to the labor room, and the doctor had told me to go home and return in a few hours. Before I left, Ruth asked me to be sure and wear a white shirt and a tie when I came back. She always liked for me to dress this way, but only now, years later, did either of us realize why. When I was dressed up, I communicated that I was in control of the situation and she felt more secure, as though she could lean on me.

As we talked about this in the group, I realized what a tremendous effect clothes had on my personality. Dressed in suit and tie, I stepped boldly into a group and took the initiative. Dressed informally in sport clothes, I hung back and hesitated to assert myself. My wife may have wanted me to be the strong man, but not all of my congregation responded favorably to my assertiveness. Something contradicted the gospel of love which respects the personhood of each individual. In suit and tie I was not very approachable, and it took the encounter group to help me see that.

Changing my pattern of dress was fun. Turtlenecks, slacks, and hushpuppies became my standard uniform unless I had a funeral, wedding, or speaking engagement. Informal clothes helped me to be a more informal person and to communicate to others a greater openness, a readiness to pause and let them be an important part of my day. The clothes don't do it by themselves; they only help my own awareness. I still have to be reminded by those who love me enough to mention it that I am rushing again, and occasionally I catch myself putting on a suit and tie to attend meetings (even breakfasts) with my brother pastors. The difference is my awareness of what is happening. I no longer take myself so seriously, and I can face these crosscurrents of the soul. Then, too, there is always an encounter group to help me face the growing edge.

Closely tied to my self-importance is my *self-propulsion*, and therein lay a further discovery. My nature has been to go into high gear while packing the power of a steamroller. I was certain that where I wanted to go, everybody ought to go. My pattern was to mow down all objections to my plans with logic, language, and enthusiasm. I discovered that this high-powered, personality-centered way of coming on left people threatened, resentful, and feeling manipulated. Any real exchange of feelings and ideas was ended.

Slowly, in the mirrors my friends provided through en-counter, I discovered my great need to become weak instead of strong. I was floored one day when a fellow with whom I had counseled for over seven years and through many crises told me how I had changed. He said I was more real now and that he felt closer to me. Then he said, "You know, Stan, you are more lovable when you are weak and don't have all the answers."

Eureka! For years I had been asking God for answers—who should head a committee or what emphasis to lift up for our congregation. Inevitably the Lord would guide me, but then I'd say, "Thanks for the tip, Lord. I'll see you later." I just wanted to do it all myself. Slowly the groups helped me see that this was no way to enable Christ's love to come into the lives of people.

At times now I half-jokingly say, "I wonder if I should have started the encounter route. It has ruined me as a minister." What I really mean is that the old-style, authoritarian, institutional way of life has been left behind and I'm not sure yet of my new life-style. To be weak and vulnerable, to be open and growing with my congregation, to allow them the freedom to minister to me, continues to produce pain along with the joy. Many members of the church resent my informality. They need the image, the sense that one man is holier than they are and can vicariously live out God's will for them. Some tasks in the institution continue to require authoritarian leadership if they are to be achieved, and this institution still holds the keys to my income and professional future.

To reconcile these conflicting motives and goals is a daily struggle, but I believe this very tension is the seedbed of truth. Daily I am reminded that if the gospel is not valid for me in my struggle, it can hardly be valid for my people in the conflicts they face. The sensitivity I am learning in the encounter groups helps me carry out God's will in my church administration and preaching and pastoral relationships. I now anticipate a lifetime of personal growth.

I know I am discovering truth, and truth must have its application or it is worthless. So I am content to be in the struggle. I trust that the Spirit of God is in it, too. I know my own weakness has led me deeper than ever before into the personal problems of my people, and together we are turning to Jesus Christ to find the answers.

BOB:

Encounter groups can be one of the best learning experiences in a person's life, particularly since they can radically affect one's inner life, as Stan has revealed. Encounter groups have demonstrated to me at a visceral level that whether I am talking about emotional maturity, self-awareness, sensitivity to others, or God-consciousness (spiritual life), growth never stops this side of death. I will always be growing and learning, unless I quit the search and let the process of decay begin. In either case I will not stay the same. There are always more "blind spots" to be uncovered, more possibilities of responding to the leading of the Holy Spirit, and better communication to be had with fellow humans.

The process is a mixture of agony and ecstasy. Great joy comes with freedom and the fulfillment of relationships established without pretense. But somehow, new discoveries never come easily. The uncovering process is seldom an "enjoyable" event. For instance, one of the most valuable things I have learned about myself is that many times I do not make a good first impression on people. The group who first expressed this said, "You came across as cold, stiff, and distant until we got to know you." A group playing "Building My House" described my house as a stone building with shutters on the windows, but with bright, warm colors inside and a merry-go-round in the backyard. They, too, were saying that their initial perception was not of the friendly, warm, and open person I thought I was. Such a disclosure doesn't do a thing for the ego, but it does provide the opportunity to alter behavior for the sake of freer communication. It also does a lot for one's patience in establishing new relationships.

Once this process of uncovering and discovering is started, life is never again as simple as it was before. The ecstasy is acquiring a new depth of meaning to life and new, vital relationships with God, self, and others. The agony is in accepting your humanness with all its shortcomings and becoming aware of painful truths of which you formerly were blissfully ignorant. The discovery of blind spots always hurts worse when you care so much and are trying to be authentic and open. Anyone entering the encounter group

53

process should be aware that learning at a deep level doesn't always feel good.

Sometimes the learning that disturbs is not about oneself, but others. After a few weeks in a group, one lady said to me, "I'm sorry I got into a group with Bill and Marge. I liked them better before I knew them so well." The question she raises is an important one. Are the surface, semi-artificial relationships to which we are accustomed safer than the in-depth relationships of an encounter group? In one sense, the answer is yes. There is always the risk that you will not like some of the things that others reveal—and others may not like what you reveal.

However, the larger question is, "Are *safe* relationships what I need or want?" The answer to that is an unqualified NO for anyone who wants to grow emotionally and spiritually. Much of the marriage counseling I have done has been to help husbands and wives quit playing it safe with each other and risk the kind of close, open relationship characterized by encounter groups. As a preacher, I rely heavily on the relationships established in encounter groups to keep my feet on the ground in my sermons. When I stand in the pulpit and look out into the eyes of persons who really know me, any tendencies to be "holier than thou" vanish. I must "preach what I live and live what I preach." When I preach judgment, it is as one of the sinners, and when I proclaim the grace of God, it is as a grateful recipient of that grace.

My firm conviction is that only the relationships which are as deep as a situation allows are truly worthwhile. If a good relationship cannot be arrived at openly, then it is better to have a poor but open relationship. Sometimes this simply means a willingness to have some people like you less than they might otherwise.

However, the depth of any relationship depends on all the parties involved. Sometimes a situation does not allow for more than a casual interaction, perhaps due to the brevity or the nature of the encounter. In other cases, the emotional defenses of another person may prevent approach. Such relationships are frustrating to anyone who has tasted the openness of encounter groups, but to reject them or demand close relationships of everyone is to violate another's integrity and the very principles of Christian encounter. Being intentionally and sensitively "shallow" with a rigid person may feel terrible, but it may also be a significant, loving act.

Finally, I must emphasize again that this is a lifelong process. If I have learned one thing from encounter groups, it is that I am in trouble as soon as I think I "have it made." As one area of life is brought under control, another is inevitably exposed. Life changes, bringing new situations and calling for new responses.

For example, our home is currently involved in that traumatic adjustment that comes when young boys "suddenly" become men. As our sons face life-determining choices (college, marriage, vocation, etc.), our relationship with them is forced to change. What once was a satisfactory way of relating is no longer adequate for the new situation.

And so, once more, the soul is exposed to struggle and doubt. In due time this situation will be resolved—only to be replaced by another. Is that pessimistic? No, that's life in all its fullness and meaning. It is not something from which to hide, but something to celebrate! For in the struggle for openness and authenticity, we are made "more than conquerors through him who loves us."

Chapter 6

□

The Power of Weakness

STAN:

Laura had grown up in the church, and her beautiful solo voice was a mainstay in the choir. But, Laura's big eyes always seemed filled with surprise or wonder or fear—which, I was not sure. Though music was her outlet for self-expression, she never really seemed to lose herself in it. I always felt she looked out on the world from a deep, quiet well, yet she never came into the world to be swept up in its tides or to be part of its heartbeat.

She married Steve, a volatile rebel whose broken home, mentally ill father, and alcoholic mother had left him rejected, angry, and afraid. They provided a lot of action in the married couples' group, with Steve lashing out and Laura speaking only when she tried to calm him down. Week after week the group absorbed his anger and prodded her silences.

One night, in the security of that fellowship, she admitted that God seemed cold and far away. In fact, her one real expression was being taken from her: She was growing unable to sing because she could no longer believe the words. The members of the group responded with love and acceptance. On another evening when she dared to reveal her aching heart, I invited her to come into the center while the group members gathered in close to touch her and pray for her. One of the other wives met her in the center and tearfully took Laura in her arms as spontaneous, verbal prayers were said. Many gentle hands touched her head and shoulders and arms, reassuring her that she was indeed loved. She learned to express her feelings openly and to accept from the group that feeling of self-worth which made the love of Jesus increasingly real.

One night a radiant Laura announced to the group, "I can sing again! God is real now! He is here, he is warm, he is love!" In the weeks following, she became a different person, sensitive to the process in the group, expressing her feelings freely, easily initiating the discussion. Her husband said she was also different at home, not so retiring. "It's like having a tiger in the house!" he exclaimed with a grin. (The next year she had grown enough to help me as coleader of a new encounter group.)

Joyce, another member of the group, was also blocked in her relationship with God and wanted the freedom in Christ she heard others talking about. At a twenty-four-hour marathon, Joyce had confessed her feeling of unworthiness; she believed she was "the worst one of us all." When we began giving verbal "gifts" to each other, Laura's eyes locked on to Joyce and whispered poignantly, "I would give you the closeness of God. . .you really are such a beautiful person." Head down, fighting back tears, Joyce struggled with the presence of God's love. The group waited in silence, sensitive to the importance of this moment.

Thirty full minutes passed—the group knit in spirit, Laura's eyes on Joyce and never wavering. Then, at last, Joyce said, "I can talk now. I feel calmer. I really do feel beautiful." She was smiling and she looked beautiful. Forgiveness had come. Christ's love had been passed from one to another. In the language of the church, Joyce was being redeemed.

During the second year that this group of married couples was meeting, Laura's husband, Steve, went through a long-term crisis. They wanted to have a child, but he felt inadequate to be a father. Deeply depressed, Steve believed he was a failure in his vocation and feared he had inherited the mental and emotional instabilities of his parents. Laura was in agony for him, but her new-found strength carried him.

The group also supported him. Sometimes Steve lay back, closed his eyes for the entire period, and said nothing. At other times he unloaded his hostility. The group learned to be sensitive to his mood, and jollied, chastised, needled, comforted, or challenged him as need be. At the end of the year he came out of the valley and confessed that the group—and Laura—had brought him through.

That summer at an Ashram he made a personal commitment of his life to Jesus Christ. Laura was nearing the end of her pregnancy, and he felt ready to take the responsibility of fatherhood. Together Steve and Laura changed their vocation. Feeling called by God, they moved many miles away from us, and from her family, to begin their new life in mission.

The encounter group in the church had made a tremendous difference in the lives of these two and consequently in their whole relationship to the world. They had found freedom to grow in the abundant life; they had been given an ongoing personal group relationship in the midst of a broken and impersonal society; they had developed a new hunger for spiritual meanings; they had provided new leadership in the church; and they had moved out with a new awareness of their mission to the world. We have seen these five specific things happening over and over again in our church as a result of the encounter groups.

(1) New dimensions in personal living

Earlier in this book, I shared the freedom and self-discovery which I have found through the encounter groups and how it affected my whole approach to the ministry. For a pastor to discover the blocks to his own effectiveness, and then to begin to work on them, may be the single most dramatic—and beneficial—effect of the groups upon the life of a church.

The effect of the groups upon the lives of individuals may never be known to the congregation at large since the encounter groups meet quietly without the published announcements which accompany most church programs. But the breakthroughs occurring through the encounter groups—persons establishing deeper relationships, finding greater freedom, having lives filled with joy and meaning—are surely a large part of our mission in the churches.

Donnell came into a group of men and women who were all either single or divorced. She had left her husband and children many years earlier, had come clear across the country, and now, in her forties, was living a frightened existence under a cloud of guilt.

Slowly the group gave her confidence as the trust level built. She tried expressing herself, and she accepted (with pain, of course) the feedback which pictured her as a mouse or a prim schoolteacher. She began to change her behavior and was able to let out her natural wit. The guilt lifted as she experienced forgiveness in the group, and she blossomed into an open, almost feisty, fun-loving person. In a few months she began attending church with a divorced man, and in due time I consecrated their marriage. They are finding fulfillment together and actively serve the church.

With the personal freedom many find in the groups, they are then able to enter new depths of personal relationships. Betty told of the terrible conflict with her office manager which made every working day miserable. Gradually, as she learned to be sensitive to the real feelings of others in the group, Betty began to see her boss as a real person, too—one to whom she needed to minister. That new perspective made her job endurable and meaningful.

Couples like Bob and Jan are learning a new awareness of

each other. One night we each made posters (or montages) of magazine pictures symbolizing our feelings and our self-image. Then husbands and wives switched posters without discussing them and shared with the group what they saw portrayed in their spouse's work.

Jan held up Bob's design—a picture of a craggy mountain and, beneath, a picture of a mountain climber looking out of his sleeping bag. She saw this as simply representing his great interest in the out-of-doors, but then Bob explained the pictures in terms of deep feelings which he had not previously expressed. The mountain was the adventurous life he wanted, but he was sheltered in his vocation as the man was sheltered in the sleeping bag (Bob referred to his job as a cocoon). Thus, Jan and Bob reached a new depth of understanding.

Single adults especially benefit from an encounter group in the church. For so many of these persons, the isolation is unbelievable, and knowing how to reach out toward fulfilling relationships is a constant problem. The long, ongoing exposure within the group slowly builds confidence in exploring new relationships and facing one's own feelings. A gentle game that involves some physical contact goes a long way in precipitating several hours of deep sharing. However, any game involving physical contact must be approached cautiously since many persons, particularly in their first exposure to encounter groups, are very sensitive about exercises and games involving touch.

Janet never sat on the floor with the other members of the singles group, but instead sat aloofly in a chair, often facing away from the group. What a happy time for us when she sat in our close circle as we held hands and prayed. Later, she smiled radiantly and said, "A year ago I couldn't do this— holding hands, touching other people." She also found the courage to quit her job, in which she felt trapped, and get one she really wanted. In other words, Janet simply came to life. It seems to me that enabling such changes to happen in people is an important part of the task of evangelism in the church. Persons are being brought to new life. Just getting a thrill out of new relationships in the group isn't the goal. I'm talking about changed lives which make new and ongoing relationships possible and which free persons to be fulfilled and to bring fulfillment to others.

Of course, some people don't make it in the groups. Even after participating for many months, some may drop out when faced with their own need to go deeper. Let us be sure these persons are free to drop out, and that the group is free to allow them this decision. Neither the group nor the individuals should feel they have failed. The time just wasn't right; they may try again later. Then, too, the time wasn't wasted; this person will never be quite the same.

One of the things, then, that happens in the church because of the groups is that lives are changed—often, delivered from bondage.

(2) New support in an impersonal society

The groups provide a place where persons can feel important and alive in an impersonal civilization. John came in one evening, kicked off his shoes, sat down on the floor next to his wife, and said, "You know, it's been a long, hot day at the shipyard. This is the one place I can come and just be myself."

Something in me leaped for joy at that remark. How important it is to have a *place*, especially in a day when the pressure of time and profit prevents openness or acceptance in the daily task of earning a living—a day when there aren't the larger families and close neighbors who in the past provided a context for honesty and experimentation in human relationships.

Too often we have assumed that Christians shouldn't have problems. This, of course, isn't true. Even Christ doesn't take us out of the human situation, and we go on hurting, growing, and making wrong decisions just like everyone else. The encounter group in the church becomes a family in the sense of an ongoing, long-term relationship within which a person can find support, chastisement, loving acceptance, and reconciliation. How desperately we all need this atmosphere in order to be whole persons!

During her early months with the group, Martha had a miscarriage, and she was unable to talk about it. She and her husband kept their grief to themselves. As the group relationship continued, however, she was able to reveal some of her feeling to others, including hostility toward her mother-in-law. The other couples offered practical suggestions on handling specific situations, and Martha was able to break through to a new acceptance of her mother-in-law. More importantly, Martha was given the wonderfully supporting knowledge that she was not alone in her problems.

Then, one week, Martha was not there. Her father, to whom she had been very close, had died unexpectedly, and she had gone to be with her mother and sisters. The group wrote her a letter, each member adding sentences of love and support. When Martha returned, she told how much the word from the group had meant. She was able to share her grief and, as she worked through the hurt of losing her father, she found her peace. Where else in today's world could she have found such ongoing support at so personal a level to carry her through the dark days? Even the church in its traditional forms of worship, projects, and potluck meals could not have provided this.

Art had suffered an emotional breakdown when he was twelve, and every spring since then a deep depression set in on him which lasted clear into the next fall. After a year in the group, he revealed this problem. As the next spring approached, he confided, "It's begun." We went through it with him. He knew he wasn't alone with his suffering. During midsummer vacation we got a card from Art's wife—"He's out of it!" The depression had lifted several months earlier was nearly upon us when Art realized he hadn't had his annual depression. When the depression did hit, it was much lighter than usual. With the group again supporting him, Art came through it well.

A second function of the groups, then, is providing ongoing support and nurture in a broken and uncaring world.

(3) New hunger for worship, prayer, and Bible study

When the encounter groups in our church began, I wondered what relationship this psychological and relational-oriented approach would have to the Christian exercises of prayer and Bible study. I decided to avoid any reference to these practices, or even to God, because small groups had incorporated prayer and theological discussions for years. Now, with new insights about interpersonal relations, I determined to see how long the group would take to move, on its own, toward God. It took two and one-half months.

Steve burst out one night, "I don't know about the rest of you, but I need to find Christ. I want to know him like some of you claim to know him!"

Immediately he found support from others who wanted the same thing, and who now found the courage to speak. That night we prayed, with hands joined around the circle. From then on, our experiences with Jesus Christ were a natural part of the group process. Assurances from some group members helped other members to know what they had missed and how to set their sights. The doubts of others helped some of us to come off our pious perches and discover we were not all that safe, either.

Becoming free in human relationships opens the door to a deepening relationship with God. The members of the encounter groups are often the ones asking for more Bible study helps outside the group. Likewise, the groups have proved to be the door through which many enter into meaningful participation in the worship services.

Spouses and friends often bring into the group persons who

have been turned off by the institutional church but are attracted to this relaxed fellowship. Slowly the trust enables them to lower their defenses, and they realize no one is pushing them to be something they are not, let alone feeling "in a short time you think to make me a Christian!" (Acts 26:28).

As the weeks pass, the stereotypes wear off. They hear the natural testimony of believers woven into an ongoing experience of life. They come to understand me as a very human being who has failures and sins, who accepts *their* failures and sins, who is not a figurehead in a black robe but a friend in a turtleneck and stocking feet sitting on the floor and expressing real feelings.

Then, one Sunday morning, I see them slip into the balcony to observe the worship service. Soon, they are participating. Often, in due time, these persons will respond to the invitation to come forward and confess Jesus Christ as Lord and Savior.

The encounter group experience enhances worship by lowering the barriers between laymen and pastors. There is a gap, believe me! A layman who met a colleague of mine coming out of the rest room stopped in his tracks and stammered, "Why, I didn't know ministers ever came in here!"

A group of single young adults with whom I began meeting had difficulty seeing me as a human being. One evening we assigned one another a color. Of eleven persons, five colored me blue or purple for royalty, and one colored me white for purity. I didn't know whether to choke or cry. I prayed that I would have the courage to let them see my real self. Then, one Sunday, we would look at each other between pulpit and pew and feel a dimension of understanding, warmth, and communication never possible before. I can speak to real needs because I am more aware of real needs. I can speak more freely, less oratorically, because I have learned this communicates better, and I trust the Holy Spirit more than my oratory. My listeners are hearing the Spirit speak to their condition more than before because they are hearing him through a real person.

Another change brought by the groups (and encouraged by the contemporary scene) is conscious planning for more congregational participation. I have become more aware of the need to involve the congregation in real encounter with the gospel and with each other. I can no longer allow them to be spectators, and group members will no longer be content with such a role.

At the more traditional Sunday morning service we have involved the congregation in greeting exchanges, community seasons of prayer, dialogue times for sharing how Christian mission is carried out in one's workaday life, and a variety of litanies.

The contemporary worship service is, of course, a more obvious time for public experiences along these lines. Too often what is advertised as "contemporary worship" is really a repeat of the old forms merely using new words, new songs, and throwing in a few new instruments (mainly guitars). In our experience the truly contemporary service requires a whole new form of involvement by the congregation.

We have been developing this on a regular basis on Sunday evenings. Young and old alike come informally dressed. The music includes organ and piano, augmented by guitar, drums, tambourines, mouth organ, and whatever else anyone can play and make a joyful noise to the Lord.

Pastors, music leaders, sound-room technicians, and ushers all meet together to pray about the service and share where we are "now." Then, during the service we take the basic elements of worship and the planned special music and fit them into a general sequence which often is altered as we get into it. There is freedom for the Spirit to move, and since all leaders are prayerfully sharing a team relationship, the Lord

65

usually dovetails the events into a perfect whole. It is a happening, with the emphasis on celebration, openness, and commitment to Christ.

Above all, we try to keep Christ preeminent. The service rarely fails to "come off"; usually it is an unforgettable experience in worship and personal involvement made possible by the new style of life and ministry which the groups have brought to our congregation.

(4) New resources for leadership

Another effect is the development of new leaders for traditional church tasks.

"Worship is 'glockey'!" said Sally in one group. She didn't like the music, the sermon, or anything else. No one told her she was wrong—that's how she felt! But over the months, something happened to Sally's feelings and perceptions. One night she said, "You know, worship is getting less 'glockey' all the time." Eventually, it grew so exciting that she volunteered to chair the worship committee where she worked diligently to make the services more meaningful and personal. Since that time she has given valuable leadership in many areas of her church's ministry.

The encounter groups do not take on projects or promote causes. That would divert attention from the real things that are happening to people in the groups. At the outset, I worried about this, knowing as I did that service in mission is a prime calling of Christians. But after the group movement in our church began to mature, a beautiful thing happened: Members began asking for jobs and volunteering for tasks. When I grew bolder and asked members to fill leadership and teaching positions, they joyfully accepted.

I was careful not to manipulate. I casually spoke of needs and did not press for acceptance. (I had learned my lesson earlier about using my office and personality and clever salesmanship to secure a yes.) For years the older leaders have prayed for young leadership, and now this is happening.

These new officers and teachers are so grateful to the church for their life-changing experiences and their new joy in living that they are eager to share of themselves. Furthermore, their eyes have been opened to a new awareness of their mission potential. Awareness of self has given them confidence; awareness of others has given them vision; awareness of God has given them strength.

(5) New response to the world

The type of program these new leaders are emphasizing is different from programs of the past. Group members have discovered that Christ is *in* the world and that the place to serve him is *out there*.

While I'm excited about this, I also feel sadness for those older members who feel deserted. They look suspiciously on the encounter groups and ask, "Why don't those young people get involved in church work and not just live for themselves?" This complaint reflects the reality of the revolution in the church and the difficulty the "old-timers" and "pillars" have in understanding the new style of Christian life. The old style was measured by involvement in "church work": meetings, committees, kitchen service, ushering, bazaars, handiwork around the property, money pledged. Young members are less interested in these expressions for their faith.

In fact, by the time the children of younger members are grown, there may be very few church properties. The Christian life for them is not the maintenance of old structures or the promotion of a building-centered and family-centered club. The church is not the *place* for a social outlet, entertainment, or status-building. Young people haven't time for the things which still seem important to older members, like having "successful" programs with large audiences, or electing officers for innumerable boards and classes.

I believe we are seeing the emergence of a generation of Christians for whom faith is deeply relevant in *every* phase of life or not at all. They measure Christian involvement by a Christlike life-style in their vocations, homes, neighborhoods, and communities. After that is done, there is no time oι, energy left for work "down at the church."

This is not to say that either approach is wrong, but that God's Spirit is leading in a change of format. The older members will continue what for them is the most meaningful expression of their faith; the younger members will develop a style which best expresses their faith. For a while, both will continue side by side. In time, as the older folks pass away, the familiar forms of church work will pass away—which is all right, because these young people *are* involved in Christ's mission, often on a more full-time basis than their elders ever were. Their theater of operation is the world, not the church property.

One of our older workers said, "But who will raise the ten thousand dollars each year if the work of the women's group is not carried on?" The answer is strange: probably nobody! Rather, ten thousand dollars worth of effort will be invested in living and witnessing for Jesus in countless corners of the community. If young Christians were working "down at the church," they couldn't be giving themselves out there.

Furthermore, the traditional forms of "mission" and hierarchy which that ten thousand dollars has paid for will be forced to change. Another trauma! But I am convinced that God is working in these events. The encounter group, as much or more than any other factor, will encourage this new direction.

It is an exciting day to be in the church—and to be the church!

Chapter 7

□

That None May Boast

BOB and STAN:

The moment of truth for any new thought comes when theory is translated into practice. To say that a church's ministry will include encounter groups sounds exciting, even a little avant-garde. To say that much of the traditional ministerial role will be abandoned and the congregational busywork directed into a new form sounds adventurous. But, when the time comes to carry out such ideas, one's real emotion is more likely to be "chicken fever." It isn't easy to let go of the familiar and reach out for the unknown, especially when you are asking other people to risk with you.

Risk is a good word to describe what we have learned about encounter groups as we have moved from theory to practice. Any minister takes a chance when he begins freeing people from old thought patterns, old guilts, old images of him as a person and pastor. When people become free to discover and express themselves, and feel an inherent sense of value and acceptance, they are not nearly so "manageable" as before.

The pastor may well find himself empathizing with the ship's captain in the cartoon. The captain is walking the plank. As the crew cheers and he plunges off into the sea, he says, "Where I made my mistake was in calling for a vote."

The real question for any pastor is, "What is more in keeping with the gospel—an institution that is easy to manage, or people finding new freedom to live a full life?" If the answer is people, there is risk.

The following key observations have evolved from our experiences with groups. We offer them here in the hope that they will benefit pastors and laymen who are considering the encounter style of ministry. Please understand that these are not iron-clad rules for conducting groups; we are simply sharing with you what was true for us.

The local church is an ideal setting for encounter groups

Encounter groups have much to offer the church. Conversely, the church can offer invaluable benefits to encounter groups. As we said in the preface, "encounter" denotes a dimension of depth in the interaction between persons in the group, an interaction characterized by such elements as openness, loving honesty, acceptance, risking, and testing. Significantly, the encounter between persons in the group parallels the encounter between God and man, thus giving a spiritual validity to the experience.

When the local church is the setting, the spiritual validity of encounter groups is reinforced, since the groups are more easily given a Christ-centered context—that is, an atmosphere of love, acceptance, and long-term fellowship. Christ-centered groups in the church allow the participants to build a love and trust of each other that can only happen over the months and years. In the family structure that the local church provides, persons can seek the common good as well as personal growth. Committed to a common discipline, they know that they must live with each other and with the results of the group experience in the broader context of the whole church fellowship.

There is real power in having persons working together in

the same areas of the church's ministry after their mutual communication and understanding have been refined in the fires of an encounter group experience. Such persons, between them, have remarkably few misunderstandings or disappointed expectations. There is power, too, in the fellowship of being together in worship and study as well as in the group experience. If, during an encounter group session, two people have not worked out a conflict, they may resolve their "unfinished business" when they come together in other church activities.

The church also encourages encounter groups to confront eternal values and issues. When persons meet in a context that includes the meaning of life, death, love, etc., encounter becomes all the more significant. The church contributes a long-term setting, shared worship experiences, sacraments, and service opportunities, making it an ideal setting for this movement.

Time and numbers are important considerations

The questions of time and numbers have a strong bearing on the success of an encounter group ministry. We do not espouse hard and fast rules. A chance encounter of a few minutes may change a life, but this is not the norm. We are suggesting here guidelines which have proved beneficial in many instances. To some degree they are safeguards against traps into which many small groups have fallen.

TIME: The duration of individual encounter groups varies widely. We have found that asking persons for a twelve-week commitment when a group forms allows time for the group to work through some of the common formative problems and become "set." It also allows the leader and participants a terminal point at which they can end the group, if they wish, without any feelings of failure. Having a set duration attracts some persons who would avoid an open-ended group and usually results in a deeper commitment to regular attendance. It is important that the group leader keep faith with the termination date, allowing the group to decide freely whether or not to continue.

Because of the nature of encounter group interaction, a group needs to meet regularly on a weekly basis. Groups that meet less often or have periodic interruptions will inevitably be shallow and ineffective.

There is no firm rule for session length. Ninety minutes is workable *if* the participants arrive on time and get down to business. Scheduling less than ninety minutes is almost sure to be frustrating, and two hours offers the temptation to waste time.

The group leader judges how rigidly the closing time will be observed. On occasion, stopping the interaction just because time is up would be almost cruel, but it is also true that some groups tend to save the real "business" for the last ten minutes, staying shallow and defensive through the early going. In that case, calling a halt at the appointed time encourages them to open up sooner.

Family schedules, child care, and work schedules must also be considered. If a person continually has to leave ahead of the rest of the group, he may feel left out and be unable to open up fully.

NUMBERS: Successful groups vary greatly in size; however, the ideal range is eight to twelve persons—with a minimum of five and a maximum of fifteen. Regularity is a critical factor of any encounter group, and the percentage of absenteeism must be kept very low.

Another consideration is the number of groups that one person should lead. The correct starting point for anyone is *one* group. The level of concentration and emotional involvement required to be an effective leader can be exhausting if too many groups are attempted at once. Under such "group fatigue," one's effectiveness diminishes rapidly. Only a person with extensive training and experience should consider taking on more than one group.

The physical setting is important

Informality is an intrinsic element of any encounter group meeting. With a little careful planning, the physical setting can help create an atmosphere of relaxed openness. The best setting is a room at the church, perhaps in the educational building designed and designated as a "group room." Encounter groups in the sanctuary are *verboten* because the setting is not conducive to good group dynamics. Ideal furnishings are: carpeted floors with padding thick enough for comfortable sitting; throw pillows or cushions; comfortable chairs or couches; and ever-ready coffee pot and/or soft-drink cooler. (But be wary of taking formal time-outs for refreshments.) Whatever room is used should have an air of intimacy and privacy— for example, a room that is too large feels "cold" and inhibits sharing. Drape any windows opening onto a street or hallway.

Nursery facilities should be sufficiently distant so that parents are not distracted by children's cries.

An ideal setting rarely exists; however, it is surprising what can be accomplished with a little ingenuity and effort.

A clear "contract" for encounter must be established

It is absolutely essential that persons coming into the experience clearly understand the goals and procedures. Some churches have had unhappy experiences caused by vague publicity, or by introducing an encounter-type event without sufficient notice. One church, for example, gathered people for membership training and then involved them in sensitivity games and other encounter techniques. The results were not good!

The firm rule is *no surprises*! Publicity should be explicit about *goals*, *size limitations*, *duration*, and *procedures* (don't let someone enter a group thinking it is a prayer, discussion, or fellowship group). We establish a *psychological contract* with the participants—everyone knows generally what to expect and what will be expected of him. This doesn't mean that a person can't drop out if the experience proves too threatening, but at least he has assumed responsibility for his participation.

When a group comes together, the members will quickly form a "group contract" to relate with each other in a new way. Upon that "contract" the group begins to build mutual trust and confidence. For that reason, *new persons should not be added after the second or third meeting.* The exception is when several persons drop out, making the group too small. However, persons should be added only with the previous consent of all group members.

Using church facilities is preferred because:

—this clearly identifies the encounter group as a church event.

—learning to be relaxed and open in a church building is a fringe benefit.

—everyone meets on neutral ground.

—child care can be provided in a facility designed for this purpose.

If church facilities are unavailable, a home is an excellent alternative. Using the same home each week enables the participants to feel familiar with the surroundings. The hosts set the pace for being informal, encouraging others to follow their example in the early gatherings of the group. When the meeting is in a home, child care should be arranged in another home or at the church.

Participants should have something in common

Ideally, members of long-term encounter groups share some common concerns. Married couples, housewives, vocational groupings, single adults, youth, servicemen's wives, etc., are the kinds of groupings that seem to work best. At some major point in their lives, the members need some common ground. Church cross-section groups almost invariably prove frustrating and short-lived.

Groups also seem to function best when the participants

are relatively the same age. This is more true for ongoing encounter groups than for short-term or weekend events. The following chart indicates the general responses of various age and interest groupings:

Group	Response
Junior high youth (12–14)	Tend to be too self-conscious, and attention span is often too short for effective use. Encounter principles applicable in special settings.
Senior high youth (15–18) and college-age youth (18–21)	Usually respond well with great flexibility. Their need to share feelings honestly with someone and to find acceptance in peer group is many times almost desperate. Offers pastor an excellent opportunity to get close to youth in the church.
Young adults (single and married, in twenties and thirties.)	Seem to gain the most from the experience. Young married couples almost always respond extremely well to encounter groups. The openness and clear communication between persons can provide a lifelong style of relating.
Middle-aged adults (forties and early fifties)	Often find it difficult to stay with an experience that is bound to be so revealing. (Whether this will hold true in subsequent generations remains to be seen.) These persons can be very defensive;

	will often try to alter the group format to accommodate chatting or social activities. They apparently are the group hurting the worst inwardly, but have the hardest time opening up.
Older adults (late fifties and over)	Occasionally will begin an encounter group experience, but seldom go more than a few weeks. Again, encounter principles can be applied to a special situation with good results. (There are exceptions: One lady who has been a vital part of an encounter group for some time is over seventy.)

One other important factor: *persons with severe or disabling emotional problems should not be grouped together*. In fact, if someone is unable to deal effectively with reality, or is severely troubled with emotional problems, it is unwise to put him in a group at all. In such cases, the proper act of concern is for the pastor to make a referral to a competent psychologist or psychiatrist, unless he feels competent to handle the necessary counseling himself on a private basis. However, every pastor must be aware of his own limitations and know when to make a referral.

The problem which occasionally arises, of course, is that someone's severe problem is discovered *after* he is in a group. This presents a different and difficult situation. If the group leader is the pastor, he can often convince the person that private counseling would be more beneficial. In most cases, such an offer will be accepted. If the group leader is a layman, he will have to consult with the pastor and together they must decide whether the pastor will take on the disturbed person or make a referral.

This is also part of the reason for starting groups with a predetermined duration—it provides a useful safety valve. The group is disbanded on the appointed date, then the others can re-form after private counseling is arranged for the troubled person. Once in a while, it becomes necessary for the person who is responsible for a church's encounter group ministry simply to remove someone from a group. However, this should be done only when all other avenues have been exhausted.

Encounter groups are not therapy groups

Everyone in the church needs to understand that encounter groups are not therapy groups. In the first place, usually the pastor or other leader isn't a professional psychologist. And second, the purpose of encounter groups is not problem-solving, but growing in self-awareness and sensitivity to other persons. There is a vital difference between a therapy group and a group that is therapeutic. Every group in the church should be therapeutic—that is, upbuilding, strengthening, supportive.

Encounter groups are for "normal" people who want to grow emotionally and spiritually. Held in more of an educational than a therapy setting, they avoid the harsh, attacking kind of interaction characteristic of therapy groups. The honesty sought in encounter groups is *loving* honesty; raw truth is tempered with love and sensitivity to others. The concept of feedback (see chapter 8) is used in all interaction to minimize judgmental feelings and expressions. The leader is not a therapist and the participants are not patients. Everyone is in it together to learn and to grow as persons.

Encounter group "cop-outs" must be avoided

In avoiding the therapy-group trap, it is easy to make a mistake at the other end of the spectrum. Encounter groups are not discussion, prayer, or social groups. To let an encounter group drift into any of these categories is a cop-out on the contract for encounter.

The leader is responsible for keeping the group from concentrating on a topic and having an intellectual exchange around it. Some people (especially the forty-plus crowd) tend to do this as a defense against opening themselves up. The same is true of approaching interaction with "The Bible says. . ." There is a place for intellectual discussion of important issues and there is a place for Bible study, but the encounter group is *not* the place for either! Personal interaction at a feeling level is the "stuff" of encounter groups.

Prayer does have a place in encounter groups, but it, too, can become a means of avoiding the threat of openness. It is far too easy to slip into "Let's pray about it" instead of facing honest feelings in a tough situation. Prayer ceases to be useful—indeed, ceases to be prayer—when it is used as a pious frosting on threatening interaction, especially when hostile feelings are involved. Honest, meaningful, and holy conversation with God can grow out of true encounter between persons. Such prayer needs no encouragement—it is spontaneous and free, and it speaks to everyone at a deep level.

Probably the most tempting cop-out is socializing. The fellowship that develops is rewarding and fresh in its authenticity, and group members naturally desire to be together for some other activity. This is good. An occasional social activity helps members to learn more about each other in a different context, as well as binding them in the sharing of a common experience. However, allowing such social activities to take the place of a group meeting, or turning the social events into encounter sessions, violates the psychological contract of the group.

Encounter groups require trained leadership

As we stated in the introduction, *Folly or Power?* is an experience-oriented book, rather than a how-to manual. We reiterate here that some leadership training is imperative for anyone interested in leading a group effectively, and we hope the basic concepts and ideas included in this book will aid persons in their preparation and training.

The following are some of the professional training organizations and groups which can provide invaluable aid in developing and enhancing one's skills in group process and dynamics. The denominational headquarters of many groups can also provide lists of individuals or organizations who offer training.

Association for Creative Change (ACC)
William A. Yon, Executive Director
Route 1, Box 35A
Chelsea, Alabama 35043

(ACC, which covers the entire country, has a listing of training programs and a survey of training organizations which can be gotten upon request.)

National Training Lab Institute for Applied
   Behavior Science
1201 Sixteenth Street, N.W., Room 507
Washington, D.C. 20036

Institute for Advanced Pastoral Studies
380 Lone Pine Road
Bloomfield Hills, Michigan 48013

Mid-Atlantic Training Committee, Inc.
Suite 325
1500 Massachusetts Avenue, N.E.
Washington, D.C. 20005

Faith At Work
1000 Century Plaza
Columbia, Maryland 21044

University Associates
Box 80637
San Diego, California 92138

Rev. Dr. Kenneth Mitchell
3502 Clairemont Drive
San Diego, California 92117

Training Enterprises New Techniques
Box 1062
La Mesa, California 92041

National Council of Churches Training Laboratories
475 Riverside Drive, Room 708
New York, New York 10027

Yokefellow Institute
920 Earlham Drive
Richmond, Indiana 47374

Christian Laymen of Chicago
Hal L. Edwards, Executive Director
1444 W. 37th Street
Chicago, Illinois 60609

The leader of an encounter group needs a high level of self-awareness and openness. The crucial skill is the ability to hear the real messages being communicated within the group. Much "listening" is done with the eyes—trying to pick up the nonverbal communication of body language. The other critical need is courage—to enforce the rules of interaction (especially in the formative weeks), to trust in group process when the going gets rough, and to face the group or individuals and their hostility.

In chapter 8 are suggestions for specific actions by group leaders to facilitate encounter. The material in this chapter should be very helpful in supplementing a regular training program.

The confidence of the group must be protected

The events and feelings shared in the group must never be revealed outside the group. The basic rule is that persons are free to tell their own story outside the group, but must never betray the confidence of other members. The commitment to openness and honesty is a sacred trust; betrayal destroys the group's integrity and ends the possibility of growth. For that reason, any examples of group events used as illustrations in this book have been carefully disguised with changes in names and circumstances, or permission has been secured from the persons involved.

Encounter groups go through predictable stages of development

It is helpful for a group leader to have some idea of what to expect as an encounter group develops. Groups sometimes flounder or break up after a few weeks because they feel "flat" or have a hard time staying on the track. Knowing that these are normal and expected stages of group development can prevent a leader from calling the whole thing off. Here is an outline of typical developmental stages. (Note: These are tendencies and are not invariable.)

1. *Testing stage*—characterized by nervousness and mutual suspicion. After a few hours, though, anxiety lessens and persons begin to relax.

2. *Leader dependence*—group leans heavily on the leader to provide answers for any problems. The more the leader "takes over," the less the anxiety; however, the group will also fixate and not go deeper, making this a time of real growing pains. (If the leader does not fit the expectation, he is sure to be attacked for not "doing what he is supposed to do," but that's the price.)

3. *Family stage*—a tendency to talk about families, childhood, feelings about parents, etc. Hostile feelings are often carefully masked.

4. *Peer competition stage*—"I have the answer you need"

characterizes much of the interchange. Often, one person is singled out in the course of the meeting and the full group attention focused on him. Putting someone on the "hot seat" keeps attention off oneself. It represents an effort to win the leader's approval and to hide hostile feelings by apparent helpfulness.

5. *Play stage*—spontaneous "goofing off" can drive the leader to the point of canceling the group. Pressure is on for social activities; the group enjoys each other so much they don't want to get down to business. "Post sessions" are common as members get together after the meeting.

6. *Subgroup stage*—in groups of single persons, pairing often occurs at some point. Open resistance to real honesty and free expression of feelings may arise. The group appears flat and disinterested, with people questioning whether it should continue and intimating they are considering dropping out.

7. *Work stage*—openness and honesty are always present in the interaction, of which there is plenty. This is a mature group which will be a real growth factor in the lives of its members. Spiritual awakening and a new interest in prayer and the Bible happen frequently at this point.

The pastor must support the movement

Many pastors are wary of becoming involved in the small group movement, especially the encounter group process. We can sympathize with the *questions* and *reservations* which pastors raise, and we'd like to share some of the answers we've found.

1. **Won't the group get into some orbit beyond the pastor's control?** A pastor with this concern should ask himself some serious questions about his need to control and dominate the persons and programs of his church. Having adequately trained, skilled leadership *is* a necessity and will be discussed separately.

2. **Won't persons in small groups become susceptible to**

the "tongues" movement with the divisiveness which often accompanies that emphasis? The encounter group with its focus on personal relationships and openness seems to have no problem with glossolalia.

3. Won't the presence of small groups challenge the pastor's authority in the church? This is especially a concern if a small group begins without a pastor's participation. We are trying to help pastors understand that authoritarianism is fading in the church, as it is in society, and they can minister far more effectively through leadership based on honest, open relationships.

4. Won't participating in a group and "being himself" impair the pastor's relationships with his people? One pastor said, "People would be demoralized if preachers were completely honest. They wouldn't listen to them anymore. The people need an example." Think what he was really saying! People do need an example—of what it means to live an authentic life of openness and sensitivity to others. They don't need another pseudo-saint who is above the problems they confront.

5. Don't small groups represent a break with the familiar and tested forms of relationship and ministry? Thus, pastors who are apathetic and unwilling to change see no value in encounter groups. They just go on their way, plodding down the same old paths and going through the motions of forms that have long since lost their relevance.

If a pastor simply cannot deal with the concerns we've listed, then perhaps groups just aren't for him. There is a sense in which it is true that some are "medicine men" and some are not. If one really lacks the basic sensitivity and feel for encounter groups, all the training in the world won't help. However, for most of us the greatest obstacle is our own unwillingness to grow as persons.

The layman who gets turned on to groups needs to be aware of his pastor's feelings and to discuss the possibility of small groups in the church with him before it is discussed with anyone else. Precisely because the group should *not* be a divisive influence but rather a center of reconciling love, it seems unwise to begin any group in the congregation without the support and blessing of the pastor. In fact, with his background in pastoral counseling and his sensitivity to the feelings of people, he may be an ideal person to lead the group. Conversely, although the pastor is usually highly trained and skilled in group leadership, there may also be others in the congregation who meet the leadership qualifications. If the pastor doesn't lead the group, it is still good for him to participate because he needs the group for his own spiritual and emotional growth.

Encounter groups represent a whole new life-style

The function of encounter groups is *enabling*, that is, freeing each person to make a mature, honest decision about every important area of his life, including his response to Jesus Christ. Yet, being free isn't enough; one must also know how to use the freedom. The result of a successful encounter group, then, is a new and satisfying way of living in the present.

When people see each other's faults—they *react*. When they see each others needs—they *respond*. Encounter groups help people learn to see needs instead of faults and to respond instead of react. Thus, people who have learned to be sensitive to the needs of others make great churchmen because, in their feelings of self-understanding and acceptance, they won't play church games. When they see manipulation, they expose it, and they infuse others with their open style of Christian living. Authentic joy and love are irresistible qualities wherever they are found!

However, such openness does not come to anyone overnight. In encounter groups we are not in a hurry to get everybody "saved" in one meeting. If a group member needs a year or more to learn to trust the others enough to become honest and vulnerable, that is his privilege. The rest of the group can wait. Occasionally the group will probe, but always his right of privacy will be honored.

Openness is a matter of personal choice. Love, joy, peace, acceptance, and a sense of worth are all present in encounter. They are anyone's, just for the taking. But each one must reach out to receive in his own time and with his own ability to trust.

The style of ministry described here is a way of life. It is applicable, workable, and desirable in every setting, rural or urban, wherever people are in relationship with each other. Hopefully, more and more Christians will accept the encounter style as a way to become more open, free, joy-filled, enabling, and thus, Spirit-used.

PART THREE

"He Is the Source"

He is the source of your life in Christ Jesus, whom God made our wisdom, our righteousness and sanctification and redemption; therefore, as it is written, "Let him who boasts, boast of the Lord." (I Corinthians 1:30-31)

Chapter 8

□

Guidelines for Group Leaders

BOB and STAN:

A successful encounter group (one that has a creative influence in the lives of the participants) doesn't just happen. It is the result of careful planning and good leadership.

There is no doubt that the key figure in any encounter group is the leader. He initiates and enables interaction between group members; keeps the group on target, yet is never domineering; confronts the manipulator and protects the weak ego; watches and listens more than he speaks; and is himself willing to be vulnerable to the group. It's a tall order, but it can be handled if one is familiar with the rudiments of leadership.

Training events are becoming more plentiful in every area of the country, and, as we've said before, every person interested in leading a group should avail himself of the opportunity for such training. (See chapter 7.) Our purpose in this chapter is to share with you some guidelines which we, in our experience, have found helpful.

The guidelines which follow are divided into two categories: (1) the leader's relationship with the group, and (2) the leader's relationship with himself. Effective leadership requires skill in both directions. However, these concepts are not magical; they are useful only in developing your own natural sensitivity.

Guidelines for the leader's relationship with the group

Basic to everything that happens in an encounter group is the concept of *feedback*. It is the basis of all the interaction that takes place; it sets the tone for the group relationship, and it is the prime ingredient needed for an atmosphere of openness. Strangely enough, feedback is a concept that is virtually foreign to our daily relationships. Thus, the group leader needs to introduce the concept at the outset and to reinforce it frequently during the first few meetings or until group members catch the idea. There is a direct connection between how well the concept of feedback is established in the group and how fruitful the group experience is for the members.

Feedback helps a person consider changing his behavior by *feeding back* to him how others in the group are responding to what he does and says. It gives one information about how one affects those around him. It helps the individual who wants to learn how closely his behavior matches his intentions.

The most important part of feedback is that it is *descriptive* rather than *evaluative*. One person says to another, "You talk too much"; or says of another, "He's too phony." Such statements are evaluations, that is, judgments of another person's value. They are neither helpful for the one addressed, nor healthy for the one who speaks. After all, think how defensive we become when we feel judged.

By contrast, feedback reduces the need for defensive reactions because it does *not* evaluate; it only describes what the observer sees and how he is feeling about it (which means that the observer needs to identify what is "going on" inside himself). Instead of "you talk too much," a feedback statement might be, "George, I'm feeling frustrated about the amount of talking you're doing in the group. For this encounter to be a good experience, I need to get my feelings straight with you. Possibly the problem is what I brought with me tonight. Can we talk about this?"

Here, the giver of feedback describes what he has observed and shares his feelings about it. Note that there is no evaluation, only a description of a problem in communication between the speaker and George. The problem might belong to George, but it also might belong to the speaker (who perhaps feels a sense of competition with George). One of the "magic phrases" of feedback is "it seems to me" (or words to that effect)—not "you are."

To be most helpful, *feedback should be specific, not general.* Closely related to this is the matter of timing. *Feedback is most useful when communicated at the earliest opportunity after the given behavior.* However, this will also depend on the person's willingness to hear it, on support available from others, and on the time remaining in the session.

To be helpful, feedback must always take into account the needs of the receiver as well as the giver. If we give feedback only to serve our own needs, it can be quite destructive. The criterion is not "raw" honesty, but loving honesty—that which considers the needs and feelings of the receiver. The more one is committed to self-awareness and openness, the more responsibility he has to be sensitive to the personhood of others.

Feedback is always directed toward behavior over which the receiver has some control. Frustration is only increased when a person is reminded of some shortcoming about which he can do nothing.

Finally, check the feedback to ensure clear communication. Communication can be amazingly difficult, even when everyone involved is really working at it. One way to check is to have the receiver rephrase the feedback he has received to see if it corresponds to what the giver had in mind. Note that in the illustration used, the feedback is addressed directly to the person for whom it was intended.

Note also how vulnerable the one who gave the feedback made himself. This willingness to risk on the part of the giver allows the receiver to hear with a minimum of defensiveness.

The same standards apply to positive feedback. "You're a great guy" doesn't mean as much as "I really like the way you seem to give your full attention to people when they are talking with you."

Here again are the important criteria:

- Feedback is descriptive rather than evaluative.
- It is specific rather than general.
- It is well-timed.
- It considers the needs of the receiver as well as the giver.
- It is directed toward behavior over which the receiver has some control.
- It is checked to ensure clear communication.

The leader needs to be sensitive to many kinds of communication. The words spoken between group members are only a part of the messages they are sending out. The voice tone is important. Is the ·speaker nervous? Does his voice convey deep emotional feelings while he speaks words that are light and airy?

In one group, a girl talked about a serious problem in an offhand way. When someone asked her what she would do if things didn't work out the way she wanted them to, she laughingly said, "Oh, I could always jump off a cliff."

The leader took her hands and said, "Kitty, I am bothered because you are laughing about something that doesn't seem funny, and there doesn't seem to be any joy in your laughter."

The girl began to cry. She sat down on the floor and poured out the account of two previous suicide attempts (which the group had accepted as accidents) and a very real plan for another try. Because someone heard and a group cared, she was able to choose another means of facing the problem.

Other persons will interject certain words or phrases into their sentences only when they are nervous or perhaps unsure of themselves. "You know," "uhh," "right?" are examples of such expressions.

Withdrawal is a very important communication for the leader to spot. It may signal a feeling of rejection, hostility, fear, or any number of other emotions, all of which block involvement and growth. Withdrawal is difficult to describe and, at times, to see. It may be as obvious as someone getting up and leaving, or sitting back and closing his eyes, or turning his back on the group.

However, it may also be quite subtle. Intellectualizing is a form of withdrawal because it puts the interaction on a "head" level and off of feelings. When someone wants to discuss the "problems of the church," he is really wanting to avoid the personal interaction of the here and now. Persons sometimes suddenly want to change the group format, meet less often, or go out to a show. Such efforts are ways of withdrawing from the business of encountering and growing.

Whatever form it takes, withdrawal is difficult to deal with because the one withdrawing is very defensive. For example, in one group Hal inevitably lay back and went to sleep, night after night for a year! The leader verbally acknowledged that this was acceptable to him, if that's where Hal was. However, he also let Hal know that he hoped the time would come when he would feel like staying awake and be able to take a more active role in the group.

At one point, the leader said to Hal, "I want to affirm your right to sleep if you must, but I also want you to know that I feel rejected when you do this." In time Hal was able to overcome this obvious withdrawal and actively participate in the group.

It is usually up to the leader, especially in the early stages, to give the kind of feedback to the one who is withdrawing that will be the most helpful. The leader should remember that each person is privileged to remain silent if he wishes, as long as he and the group are aware of what they are doing. But no one is privileged to intellectualize or to change the encounter format to a social or discussion style.

A group session began one evening with everyone being flippant and shallow, carefully staying away from personal sharing. After several minutes, the leader interrupted and said, "Let's draw a line across this evening so far. What is happening? Do you like the feeling you have about what we are doing?" The level of interaction was immediately changed, and much honest sharing took place.

Sometimes the most important communication is not a spoken word, but a nonverbal message. In every group some will sit curled up, arms crossed over the chest, knees pulled up or legs crossed—possibly a sign of defensiveness or an unwillingness to be vulnerable. Others will sprawl easily on the floor or sit back in a relaxed manner, saying to all, "I am here and I'm comfortable with you." Also, it is important to note whether group members look at the person to whom they are speaking. Can they make physical contact if it seems to be called for?

A group of teenage boys found themselves side by side in a group when they were called upon to join hands. After much nervous laughter, attempts to leave, and shoving each other around, the best they could do was interlock their little fingers. As the leader fed back to them what he had observed, they were able to verbalize their deep-seated fears of homosexuality and uncertainty about the male role in society (all were from broken homes). The theological significance of this experience becomes evident when one considers the images these young men must have had when a well-meaning Christian invited them to "put your hand in Jesus' hands" or "surrender yourself to God your Father."

The leader needs to have in mind some idea about the general needs that will be brought to any interaction. Knowing these needs at least generally helps the leader to understand the behavior of the participants and to measure the changes taking place.

One such theory of needs which we have found to be helpful is described by William C. Schutz in his book *Joy: Expanding Human Awareness*. Schutz contends that persons have three basic needs from and toward other people: *inclusion, control,* and *affection.*

Inclusion refers to the need to be with people and to be alone. In the life of a group, it has a great deal of influence in the process of formation. How much does a person want to be in the group? How much does he want to include others? The person with a low level of inclusion is generally called an introvert. The person with a very high need in this area is an extrovert. However, Schutz points out that the basic anxiety is the same in both cases—the feeling that one is worthless and will be ignored by the group. What the leader looks for is the participants' growth toward a balance wherein they are at home in the group, yet not dependent upon it; where they are free to be a high or a low participant in a given session without anxiety; and where they want the others to be involved, but recognize their freedom to stay out.

Control, according to Schutz, means (1) the need to have enough power to lead others, and (2) the ability to relinquish enough control so that one can lean on others to teach, guide, and/or be supportive. The extremes here are the autocrat, who wants to dominate the life of the group, and the "abdicrat," who wants no responsibility for the group's future. Again, Schutz points out that the underlying problem is the same: feelings of being incapable and a lack of trust in others. Of course, the participant's goal is to be comfortable either giving direction to the group or following the lead of others. At that point, the person feels capable and responsible, having trust and respect for the others.

Schutz says the need for *affection* means giving and receiving enough love, warmth, and tenderness so that a person feels worthwhile, yet is free to relate without deep involvement if the situation calls for it. The person with too little affection avoids all close ties; he is distant, impersonal, reserved. He feels unloved and distrusts the affection of others. Inwardly, he is convinced that if people get to know him well, they will discover how unlovable he really is.

The "overpersonal" person wants everyone to like him and be close to him. He works hard at not offending anyone. When confrontation occurs between people in the group, he becomes anxious and uncomfortable. Often he will try to smooth over the conflict, with no effort to resolve the problem. He continually seeks "proof" of the group's love and acceptance of him.

The leader guides the group toward a wholeness in which close personal relationships present no problem, but the person can also relate comfortably at a shallow level. He wants to be liked, but can handle it if he is not. He is free to embrace others physically and emotionally, but respects the need of another for distance.

Of necessity, this has been an all-too-brief description of a carefully developed theory. For a comprehensive statement see *Joy: Expanding Human Awareness* by William C. Schutz. Let us just say here that the leader will enhance his group skills if he is familiar with and applies principles, such as inclusion, control, and affection to the groups he leads.

Encounter groups are not therapy groups. By therapy group we mean one directed by a skilled professional leader. In such groups the leader often asks probing questions which open the depths of the human psyche, and frequently there is intense, hostile interaction between participants that requires the professional skills of the leader. The leader of an encounter group, on the other hand, is not a "therapist," and the group members are not "patients." Together, they are a group of "normal" people who are seeking to grow in their self-understanding and in their ability to have constructive relationships with others.

From the leader's standpoint, this principle has its greatest importance when dealing with the way in which participants interact with each other. For this reason, we have gone into great detail about the concept of feedback. However, it is imperative for all participants to understand from the beginning that no one's personhood will ever be violated in the group. There will be no group attacks, no "peeling" of an ego, nobody "sitting on the hot seat" against his will. The last word on whether a person is brought into the group's interaction belongs to that individual.

The leader is responsible for checking the feelings of anyone who is "on the spot" to see if he is willing to go on. The leader must also be willing to step in and stop the interaction when he senses that someone has had enough or that a weak ego is being strained too far. Our experience shows that when this principle is operative, persons learn about the meaning of grace at a profound level—and this, after all, is surely a major task of the Christian church.

The other side of knowing when to stop the group's interaction is knowing when and how to initiate or facilitate encounter. For this purpose, the leader needs a supply of techniques or games at his disposal. Appendix 1 contains a compilation and a short bibliography.

The term "games" probably needs some definition, since it is used in several different ways in various fields. Games here have no connection with the destructive interaction described by Eric Berne in *Games People Play*; they are, in fact, used to break down game-playing in the Berneian sense. Neither are we referring to the simulation games used in the field of organizational development.

Games, as described in this book, refer to techniques which either *help persons to dramatize internal feelings*, thus getting them out front where they can be dealt with openly, or *facilitate interaction around some need* (such as inclusion, control, affection). Games counteract intellectual discussions and help the group through flat spots. They are, of course, essential in getting the group started. The group leader needs to become familiar with a basic set of games and then experiment until he feels confident using them. One of the leader's goals is to become so sensitive to his group that he can improvise games on the spot.

The final guideline for leadership is one that some people may feel deserves a place at the beginning instead of the end. That is, *the leader needs to be alert for the natural expression of faith by members of the group*. The encounter groups of which we write are Christ-centered, church-related groups. The wholeness of persons—which is the goal of these groups —includes that realm usually referred to as one's "spiritual life." However, we are deliberately de-emphasizing it here. An effective leader of an encounter group makes every effort not to manipulate the group interaction; neither does he manipulate the Christian commitments of the group. For that reason, the leader never introduces a "religious" atmosphere. Too many people simply have too many stereotyped concepts, most of which inhibit rather than facilitate spiritual and emotional growth. One of the fastest ways to end interaction and halt meaningful encounter is for the leader to say, "Let us pray. . ." This and other typical "churchy" actions by the leader (such as couching the interaction in a "religious" vocabulary, inserting numerous biblical references, or including devotions as a part of the meeting) will do nothing but hold back the growth of the participants. The leader is responsible for avoiding such "religious cop-outs."

Having said that, we hasten to add that one of the tasty fruits of an encounter group is the blossoming of new, mature, and vital spiritual experiences in many of those who participate, including the leader. The form of expression may be, and often is, different, but it is still valid. The point here is to remind leaders that although the leader does not introduce "religious" activities, he must be alert for and respond to the expressions of faith which inevitably evolve. The leader helps individuals and the group to explore their emerging spiritual feelings, again in the here and now, and in terms of personal experience, not dogmatic, doctrinaire statements. Such exploration may also take a while. Encounter groups are not instant salvation.

(The word "religious" is put in quotation marks to indicate a certain style and atmosphere commonly associated with church groups and formal worship services. We believe that the atmosphere of openness and acceptance which characterizes an encounter group is truly religious in the sense of being true to the way of Jesus Christ and the early church.)

At the close of an especially meaningful session, someone may remark how prayerful it seemed or how much they felt the presence of Christ in the group. At such a time, exploring the meaning of prayer and/or allowing the opportunity for expressions of faith will provide the group with a worship experience that all will treasure. The time to join in offering prayers to God comes in every group, and when it does, no one has to force it. Once a leader has heard the depth and the honesty of prayer in this setting, he will have no more questions about his way of handling the group's religious experiences.

Guidelines for the leader's relationship with himself

An effective leader needs skill in relating to himself as well as his group. The person who is not reasonably aware of his own needs, motivations, limitations, and hang-ups can do a group more harm than good. For this reason, a person wishing to lead a group needs to have previous experience as a member of a group. If this cannot be arranged, the leader may appoint a co-leader to observe and, afterward, to help evaluate the session and the leadership.

There are an increasing number of opportunities for training and skills development. Many denominations now offer training events, and a number of seminaries have courses available. We encourage every pastor and every layman who is interested in groups to avail himself of all the training he can get. See chapter 7 for further information on training opportunities.

The openness which is so important to an encounter group

begins with the leader. He must be willing to be vulnerable to the group and lead from weakness, not from strength. His frailties are the first to be exposed because he is aware of them, has accepted them, and is willing for others to know him just as he is. A pastor who is going to lead an encounter group with his laymen needs to consider this very carefully. In the language of psychology, leading an encounter group requires an adequate amount of ego strength. Leader: know yourself—accept yourself—trust your feelings!

This will be difficult, though, when the leader faces rejection. Rejection challenges one's concept of self, and it's quite likely that an encounter group leader will confront rejection by the group in some form at some time. A leader can't be "chicken" about keeping the group down to business or about confronting deviant behavior, even though doing so won't make him popular. Therefore, a leader is wise to come to terms with his feelings about being rejected and handling hostility before entering the arena of encounter group leadership.

Besides trusting himself, the leader needs to trust the process of encounter groups. This book is an attempt to provide some printed basis for such trust, but the best source is undoubtedly experience. Once a leader has gone through the process—has felt the anxiety and joy, the frustration and fulfillment—he will be much more ready to do it again. Whether group participants are really confronting one another or are caught in a dead calm, the leader can take comfort in knowing that such actions are a normal part of the process. One key point for the leader is this: *No session is a failure provided the group sticks to the encounter process!* Whatever happens in the course of the meeting just happens. It isn't necessary that sessions close with all differences settled and everyone feeling petted and warm. Rather, unfinished business is simply picked up at the next session.

If the group doesn't respond to a game—*that* becomes the focus of the session. The leader simply has to trust the group process and "hang loose." More often than not, the meeting will not go as planned. Perhaps a participant will come with something on his mind that he needs to get out in front of the group. Or, some significant feeling will be triggered by a game. In any case, it is useless to go on until the business at hand is settled.

The leader feeds back what he observes, sees that the group does not drift into a problem-solving discussion, and lets them go where they will. The leader's agenda is openness, honesty, acceptance, and encounter; the subject matter (content) is always secondary. This is group business, but it begins within the leader. His commitment and trust in the group process lead the way.

One final note. In the early life of a group, most of the interaction tends to center on the leader. Questions are addressed to him, his approval of members' statements is sought. If the leader isn't alert, a communication pattern will develop in which there is little interaction between group members without reference to the leader. In this situation, encounter is impossible and the pervading feeling will be frustration.

Ideally, the interaction is shared and experienced by all. The leader guides but doesn't dominate. His leadership is group-centered. He encourages participants to share that leadership and to have ownership in all that takes place in the life of the group. Since it is their group, they are responsible with the leader for its outcome.

How close a group comes to the ideal pattern depends heavily upon how free the leader is to trust the process and the group. This is an internal matter resting in the soul of the leader.

Chapter 9

□

A Place to Begin

STAN and BOB:

How do you begin an encounter group in your church? One pastor, before proceeding to establish a group, sought the approval of his official board. Instead, he got an argument derogatory of encounter and sensitivity groups. Most of the opinions were based on hearsay. Someone had read sensational stories of immoralities involving "touch groups." Someone else attacked the encounter method, raising the specter of Communist-inspired groups breaking down a person's defenses and making them susceptible to infiltration. The pastor found it almost impossible to rebuke such emotional accusations. Though his own experience with groups had been positive, he could not recreate that experience in words for his board members.

Why should a pastor or education committee or group leader have to precipitate an official discussion about encounter groups? The best procedure is probably to go ahead and start implementing the groups. Our experience is that the spiritual depth and new leadership which filter into the congregation from the groups will in time prove that they are of value. Of course, the participants will become aware of this sooner than the congregation at large, and they can begin to report positively about their experiences.

If a group is to be started, it is important that the pastor be in favor of it. He may or may not be the leader. Since a number of churches may have lay members more skilled in group interaction than the minister, he may request one of them to serve as leader. If so, it is still desirable for the minister to participate in the encounter group.

We shall assume here that the pastor will begin the group. He assembles a list of persons who have communicated their desire to participate; meanwhile, he is praying about who will be in the group, what kind of group it will be, and his own spiritual readiness to lead it. He should also have already undergone some training experiences to prepare for leading the groups.

There are four basic ways to start.

(1) Personally speak to those on your list about their willingness to join you in a weekly encounter group. Call them together to discuss your understanding and theirs of such a group. Then begin, using the guide for the opening sessions which appears later in this chapter. For best results, have at least six other persons. With fewer than seven persons altogether, the dynamics of interpersonal relationships slow down and are less creative.

(2) Announce that there will be a public meeting for anyone interested in encounter groups. Publicity can be given in church publications, committee meetings and class meetings, and announcements from the pulpit. These announcements should summarize the philosophy of encounter groups.

When the meeting begins, the convener may describe the purpose and conduct of the groups. If possible, have persons present who can testify to the joy and growth they have found through an encounter group. To illustrate techniques, you might use feedback and demonstrate some of the dynamics. You could respond openly to someone in the group about whom you are feeling positively. For example, tell him how you are feeling appreciative of him right now because you sense his support of you. Or you might share how frightened you feel because you are afraid some people will reject you. Of course, whatever feeling you share, be certain it is honest, not a put-on.

At the conclusion, pass out individual cards and have those present indicate whether or not they would like to be in such a group. Emphasize a commitment to regular weekly attendance for at least twelve or thirteen weeks. Those who wish to join should give their age, marital status, vocation, and the time of the week they prefer to meet. Collect these cards and dismiss the meeting.

Your homework is to put together a group and find a mutually agreeable meeting time. We reiterate that for the long-term group mixing widely divergent ages and educational levels, or mixing married couples with single and divorced persons, is unwise. So is grouping a majority of people with similar vocations. Either group all those with the same vocation, or else be sure the vocational background of participants is diversified, with no more than two in the same profession.

(3) Announce a meeting of college-age persons, or couples married less than three years, or teachers who desire to be in an encounter group. In other words, announce the start of an encounter group for a specifically defined group of persons.

Personally invite those you'd like to have in the group. If enough show up to form a group or a nucleus, proceed to discuss the philosophy and expectations of encounter and arrive at a regular meeting time. If a large group turns out, you may need to register those who seriously want to proceed. Later, work out as many groups as necessary.

(4) Conduct a workshop over a period of several weeks. The advance publicity should summarize the theology and need for encounter groups, setting a specific place and time for a series of experimental meetings. Hold the series in a large room or social hall so that if more than eight or ten persons come, those attending can be divided into small

groups. For a limited time, virtually any number of persons can be directed in a large area where the leader can guide the process for them all.

After, say, three sessions over as many weeks, you can meet as a whole body, evaluate the experience, and sign up those who desire to join a permanent group. By this time, some groups may have developed such a closeness that they will want to continue as a group for another agreed period, perhaps thirteen weeks. At that time, they would decide either to disband or go on.

See appendix 2 for a more complete description of the encounter workshops.

Four beginning sessions

To help you get started, we are suggesting ways for conducting the first four sessions. Limit them to ninety minutes each, starting promptly and ending on time, unless some deeply personal sharing suggests an extension. (Always get a consensus for the extension.)

In the first session, the participants will try to get in touch with how they feel about themselves. In the second meeting they will seek to be aware of how others see them. In the third session they will experience an awareness of themselves and others in relationship to each other; finally, they will try to measure their awareness of what is happening between them.

SESSION 1

(1) If you have a carpeted room, have the group members remove their shoes on entering and be seated in a circle on the floor. If their dress is too formal or the floor isn't covered, use chairs. Suggest informal dress for future meetings. In fact, it would be wise to mention informal dress in the advance publicity about the meetings. The removal of shoes communicates intimacy and "at-homeness." If the members are new to each other, first-name tags that can be read across the circle will be helpful in the first meeting.

(2) When everyone is seated, ask each person around the circle to tell how his home was heated when he was seven years old. You will be surprised at how much information about each person this will reveal in a gentle way. Be alert for communication on how each feels about his childhood, watching facial expressions, tone of voice, and content of description.

(3) After this initial sharing, explain to the group that each is to prepare two montages. Magazines (especially those with pictorial advertisements) are laid out in the center of the floor, together with scissors, paste, and large pieces of construction paper of various colors. Each person will choose two pieces of the construction paper, in colors corresponding with his feelings. Then, without discussion (and without getting engrossed in the magazine articles), members are to leaf through and cut out pictures, words, and/or designs for their two montages. The first should symbolically express their present self-image; the second portrayal should depict what they would like to become. This process will take an hour or longer. We suggest recorded background music to ease the tension and facilitate the process. Remind the group that seeing the symbols may be hard at first, but they can begin by clipping pictures or words with which they feel an identity. The montages will shape up by trial and error as the group's feeling grows for what they are doing. Those who finish first can clean up the scraps and return the magazines to the boxes.

(4) Now gather again in the circle. Ask for volunteers to hold up their montages and share what they mean. Many will discover insights about themselves; but most of all, each person will be inviting the others into his inner life at a depth which might not be achieved in many months of abstract verbalization.

It is important that the members not criticize or make fun of one another's montages, or argue over the explanations. Each should feel that he is totally accepted by the others as he reveals insights about himself. The leader should help the group to be aware that its function is only to listen and observe.

As a variation, each person is invited to hang his montages wherever he likes. The leader should note the location to himself. What does it say about the person's self-image?

(5) Though you will probably not complete the sharing during this session, call time at the end of ninety minutes. Some members may have other obligations, and a prompt beginning and cut-off will be encouraging. Going on consensus suggests that each participant is important; never take votes and invoke rule by majority. If you agree to go beyond the set time limit, make sure they know this will not be a regular happening. See that the posters are signed. Keep them for the next session.

SESSION 2
(1) Begin by asking the group how they felt about last week's session. Allow time for each participant to respond.

(2) If anyone didn't have a chance to display and discuss his posters, place the whole lot of them in the center and ask each member to pick out his own. For a few minutes have the members reflect and recapture the mood, then continue sharing. When everyone has spoken, collect the pictures. Save them for another session months hence when it will be interesting to review them and discuss how one's self-image has changed.

(3) Now explain that the group is going to *build a house* for each one present. Do not give extensive instructions; simply explain that when a member wants to have his house built, he says, "Build me a house!" With that, he remains absolutely quiet while the group verbally constructs a house for him. Invite them to describe its architecture, floor plan, decor, furniture, windows, setting, landscape, surrounding, type of construction, etc. Emphasize that if anyone knows the real house in which a person lives, try to forget that and start afresh.

What will soon become obvious, and what you will *not* say in introducing this game, is that the group will be describing in the symbolic house how this person is coming across to them. (This exercise may start slowly, but it should pick up in freedom of expression.) Usually the group will be able to agree on how the house should appear. If the group cannot agree, then the person being discussed probably is confused about himself and unconsciously projects this confusion.

After each house is built (allow at least five to seven minutes—longer, if necessary), the subject may wish to ask clarifying questions of the group, but he may not debate the judgment of the group. You see, whereas the poster in session 1 was the individual's opportunity to share his self-image, now the house-building is the group's opportunity to share with the individual how he is coming across. Allow the group to discover this idea for themselves. If you explain ahead of time, their efforts will become too conscious and deliberate.

After each has had his house built, open the meeting for general discussion by asking the group how they felt about this. They will probably be amazed that they were able to hit so accurately upon the inner feelings, likes, and dislikes of each other. Often the elements of decor, etc., will have been described exactly as the individual would most like them to be.

SESSION 3
When the meeting begins, remind the group that in the first two sessions each person became more aware of how he feels about himself and how the group feels about him. This time you want to grow in your awareness of how you each feel in relationships with other persons. To do this, you would like to try some simple "touch" exercises in this session. Since many persons may feel threatened, explain briefly what they can expect and ask for a consensus of the group before proceeding. If some persons do object, ask them if they would

like to verbalize their feelings. However they respond, assure them that they do not have to participate in the "touch" exercises if they choose not to and that this decision will be respected by the group. Be sure shoes are off and the group is sitting in a close circle. Do not have spouses sitting next to each other.

Say to the group:

(1) "I want each of you to close your eyes and relax. Grow peaceful in the quietness. Be aware of your own body, the pressure points as you sit or lean. What does each part of your body feel like?

"Now, beginning with your toes and slowly, slowly working up to your scalp, tense your muscles. (The leader may slowly call off the parts of the body as the tensing exercise rises from toe to ankle to calf to thigh to buttocks, etc.) Once you have reached the top of your head, holding the whole body tight, reverse the process and begin relaxing, muscle by muscle from head to toe.

"Now, with eyes still closed, make your own left hand go limp. Fully support it with your right hand. Tenderly care for the limp left hand, exploring it inch by inch with your right hand. Then place both hands in your lap.

"Now place your right hand on the shoulder of the person on your right. Gently explore that shoulder with your hand."

After a full minute of this exploration, invite the group members to open their eyes and talk about how they felt. This should include how they felt as they explored the other person's shoulder and how they felt about their own shoulder being explored.

(2) "Close your eyes again, and stretch out your arms. *Feel the space* over your heads and behind your backs. Now continue to feel the space all around you. Be aware of your contact with others, or the lack of it."

After several minutes of this, ask the participants to open their eyes and talk as a group about how they felt. Notice (without naming names) that some preferred to stay in their own space, some resented others intruding, some wanted to touch those next to them but were afraid, some sought out the others and enjoyed the contact. Talk about the meaning of this for yourselves.

(3) After the brief sharing period, instruct the group in what we call *milling*.

"I want each of you to walk about the room in any direction your body takes you. In other words, do not consciously determine where you go; just relax and let your body lead. When you find a location in which you feel most comfortable, stop in that place. If your body does not feel 'right' or 'comfortable,' continue to mill about until you like where you are."

When everyone has come to a standstill, call their attention to where they are in relation to other persons. To whom are they the closest? Most distant?

(4) Now have the participants form groups of twos (called dyads), each with the person closest to him. If there is an odd number, the leader will go unpaired.

Explain that the group is going to experiment with non-verbal communication, and each dyad should sit knee to knee. (If you're on the floor, sit close, facing each other.)

Say to them: "Words so often get in the way of real communication. We use them to shield our real feelings, or we become so preoccupied with them that we miss the messages coming to us through the other person's body language.

"To begin this exercise, each of you close your eyes and reach out to your partner, placing your hands on his hands, palms on palms. Pretend that you don't know anything about this person except the touch of his hands. Now without speaking, communicate the following messages to those hands with your hands (give directions about thirty seconds apart): 'I like you. . . .I don't like you. . . .I'm afraid of you. . . .I'm fighting with you. . . .I need you. . . .I want you. . . .I want to help you. . . .goodbye.'

110

"Now talk with your partner about how you felt doing this."

After an adequate amount of time, move on to the second part of the nonverbal communication exercise.

"Face your partner so that toes and knees touch. Hold each other's hands and look deep into each other's eyes without diverting them for one minute. Do not make a sound. I will call time after one minute."

When a minute has elapsed, say to the group, "While you are still looking into each other's eyes and still holding hands, begin talking about anything you wish. Tell your partner what you see in his eyes and what they are communicating to you."

After several minutes, have the dyads turn to form one circle and invite the entire group to talk about how this exercise affected them and to share any insights they gained.

(5) Now for another experience in relating to each other.

"This time you are each going to take a vacation trip with the group. Close your eyes and let fantasy take you anywhere you wish. Be silent for five minutes or more as you imagine this good time with the group. Think how each member of the group will react to the place you have chosen."

After a given time, tell the group to "come home." Pause. Now, with eyes open, go around the circle and let each person tell about the trip he shared with the others.

(6) Finally, try the exercise known as *passing in a circle*. This will help persons to experience themselves further in relation to the others, and to discover the degree of trust they have in the group.

Procedure: The group stands in a tight circle with one member in the center. He closes his eyes, locks his knees, keeps his feet together and his entire body reasonably stiff, though not rigid. Folding his hands over his chest, he falls back, is caught by the caring hands of the group, and is tenderly passed around or across the circle at varied speeds and directions. After a few minutes of passing, he is stood in the center of the circle, enclosed tightly by the group, and then left standing alone as the group slowly moves away.

Each member of the group is offered a turn in the center. (If someone declines, the group should not insist.) Afterward, sit and let each person discuss how he felt about the experience. (Include any who may not have participated.)

(7) Invite the group to join hands in a circle, then close their eyes and imagine the love of God pouring through each of them and flowing out to each of the others. Tell them to go in their imaginations around the circle, pausing at each person to feel God's love for that one.

(8) After a few minutes, invite the group members to offer verbal prayers about the whole encounter. At the conclusion of the prayer time, the meeting is over.

SESSION 4

This fourth session may be completely nonstructured to allow for spontaneous expression and for testing the relationships developed over the past three sessions. As leader, you will enter the room and take your place as usual, only this time you will have no games to play, no beginning words, no guidance to give. Just wait in silence and see what happens. Sooner or later, some members will realize things are different this time. Someone may ask when you are going to begin, and you will respond that the group began at its regular time.

This may be difficult for the group to accept, and different reactions will appear immediately. Your part is to be real, to feed back to the members how they are coming across and how you are feeling. The dynamics will be "grist for the mill." Some previously unexpressed hostilities about the whole group process may come to the surface, perhaps hostilities toward you as leader. Will you be able to accept these feelings? Will you be able to share how *you* feel being on this spot? Perhaps some will request more games "to get us going." In fact, the group is already "going." Awareness of feelings and relationships is being experienced; opportunities for self-examination, for support of others, and for understanding are immediately present.

Allow the entire period to proceed spontaneously. Your task as leader will be to watch for the pitfalls discussed in earlier chapters. Call a halt where someone's hostilities center on another person, and insist that the hostile one take responsibility for his own feelings. Facilitate the exchange by observing how *you* are feeling about what is happening. Direct attention to abstract discussions which get away from the "here and now."

A common dodge in this situation is for several members of the group to launch a shallow conversation about something outside the group relationship, while the other group members check out emotionally. Let this go for a while and then intrude with something like, "Let's draw an imaginary line across this conversation. How do you feel about what is going on in here right now?" Inevitably, several of the silent ones, maybe even the talkers, will jump in with, "I am feeling bored (or restless, etc.)" or "I think we're off the track." With this, you are back to the "here and now" of the group experience.

Do not be afraid of silence. It is creative. The dynamics of group relationships continue during silence. Use the quiet periods to be especially sensitive to each individual in turn, to what each is saying in body language, to the feelings you are having, to "vibrations" you are picking up. Review in your mind some of the things you have learned about groups.

If a particularly intense conflict is going on between some of the group members, introduce a game you've learned (or which you create on the spot) which will help them to dramatize and resolve their feelings, or at least get them out where they can be dealt with honestly. If you suggest such a game to the group or members of it, be sure to admit beforehand your own feelings. For example, "I am sitting here feeling a lot of tension between Joe and Bill. It's making me feel uncomfortable, and I'd feel better if they'd get it out in the open. Would you two like to do something called 'The Press'?" (See *Joy: Expanding Human Awareness* by William Schutz, page 157.)

Perhaps you yourself are feeling hostile toward someone; if so, deal with the situation openly. Or perhaps you feel someone in the group has been rejected and you want to go over and sit by him, or hug him, or just tell him it's OK. Do it.

So the meeting goes, intentionally unplanned but following certain principles of encounter which will grow more obvious to you with experience. Try not to be anxious, but if you are, admit it. There is no one way. The relationship is the thing, and into the midst of your growing freedom and awareness, the Spirit of God will come. You could well use the silent periods for your own prayers—not anxious "Help me!" prayers so much as relaxed times of praise and thanksgiving for these other persons and for God's love toward you all.

Fifteen or twenty minutes before quitting time, ask the group how they feel about what happened today. An honest evaluation will help you all to get the fullest meaning out of the experience.

Chapter 10

□

This is God's Business

BOB and STAN:

Our experience with encounter groups is not unique. Other churches have formed such groups and had similar positive results. Evidence is mounting that Christian encounter groups can change the character of a congregation, affect program priorities, alter worship practices, and evoke a new relationship between a pastor and his people.

To risk such changes in the church, one must have a lot of faith in group process. For that reason, the most important thing we have learned is that encounter groups are not merely new games for people to play. There is even something much deeper here than people finding themselves and new life. *This is God's business we are about!*

The relationship of one human being with another has been God's business for a long, long time. What psychologists learned early and theologians learned late, the Bible puts in the creation narrative: man was made for relationship. The world into which Adam came was a world that was good— no pollution, no war, no thermonuclear or population bombs. Even so, life in Eden was empty. Without relationships, Adam was a misfit in a perfect world. With the advent of another person, he cried out, "This at last is bone of my bones and flesh of my flesh . . ." (Genesis 2:23). That need has not changed. Space-age humans, like their Stone-Age ancestors, are made for relationship, and without it life is empty.

However, there is risk in relationship because it has the power to create or destroy. Loving, open, authentic relationships create. Dishonest, masked, or manipulative relationships destroy. One of the most profound statements about broken relationships is in Genesis 3, one of those scriptural gems that we know to be true because it is us. When deceit fractured the good relationship of man and woman, paradise was ended. Their relationship was no longer fulfilling. The barrier that grew between them soon became a barrier to God as well. The outcome was that they became afraid and went to hide among the trees.

Today we are still afraid, still hiding, still seeking a way to find each other and God once more. One reasonable understanding of "original sin" in this day is the contagious nature of broken relationships. Openness and wholeness of character are not passed on by persons engaged in game-playing and mask-(fig leaf?) wearing. If the current dilemma of mutual alienation is to be solved, people must have a way to relearn the art of being authentic.

In *The Gift of Power* Lewis Sherrill affirmed, "The human self is formed in relationships; if it is de-formed, it is de-formed in relationships, and if it is re-formed, it is re-formed in relationships." Sherrill's formula applies equally to our alienation from God. The human experience of God is formed in relationships with other persons; if it is de-formed, it is de-formed in relationships, and if it is re-formed, it is re-formed in relationships.

It is a fact of life, from the Garden to megalopolis, that we cannot be without relationships. Neither can we be in a destructive relationship with others and remain emotionally and spiritually alive. One can know all there is to know *about* God and yet die as a person. Alienation from one's fellowman is inevitably alienation from God.

What does this say about the mission of the church? It says that many times our ministries unwittingly hurt rather than heal broken lives. Study material can become a block to personal growth; you can hide from God behind a church or a Bible as surely as Adam hid behind a tree. The very act of being "religious"—when this involves authoritarian, judgmental attitudes—can destroy Christian character.

The church's task is to bring people into a meaningful, life-changing relationship with the God we know in Jesus Christ. To do this takes more than memorized Bible verses and knowing all the do's and don'ts. It takes a shift from a content-centered, rule-learning process to a person-centered emphasis on encounter and interaction. When people encounter each other instead of a printed word, when they share feelings instead of rubbing intellects, authentic relationships are re-formed. The self becomes acceptable because it is immersed in an atmosphere of acceptance. There, too, the real encounter can happen.

In *God With Us* the late Joseph Haroutunian wrote, "...all the life I have with my fellowmen is a life I have also with Christ . . . wherever my neighbor and I are present, Christ is present with us and to us."

This is not to say that Bible study, prayer, and preaching should be eliminated or pushed to the margin of the church's interest. It simply means that these and all other church activities can be carried out in a new atmosphere of openness and loving honesty, the result being a new depth to Bible study, a whole new world of meaning in prayer, and a new freshness to preaching.

The encounter approach is for most churches a radical change in style. A pastor or layman who finds the prospect threatening can alleviate his fears by remembering that we follow the most radical One in history, whose claim upon us is the ultimate claim of the ultimate kingdom. Encounter is radical because it is original and fundamental. Of course, that touches the core of our being. Why, then, should we be surprised at a revolution in our souls? For this reason, if no

117

other, Jesus has always found the greatest response among the young. The encounter approach is no different. Now, as then, the more one is entrenched in established traditions, the more difficult and painful it is to open to change.

The goal of encounter groups is to foster a continuing re-formation in the lives of people—that is, re-forming the religion of childhood into the religion of maturity. This re-formation of the spirit happens as broken and distorted relationships are healed and made whole. But more is needed than the usual scattered, casual contacts between persons in the usual church relationship. Authentic relationships of love, trust, acceptance, and openness become possible where people gather in small groups and engage in meaningful encounter over an extended period of time.

In the intimacy of such honest seeking, the Spirit of God, who made us for relationship, is revealed. He brings new birth and leads the way into the promised land of wholeness. We find that meaning in Jesus' command: "You, therefore, must be perfect (whole), as your heavenly Father is perfect (whole)" (Matthew 5:48). God intends for every person to fulfill his own, unique potential—to be perfect—whole. The encounter group's goal is not to mass produce "model Christians," but rather to free people to find their own distinctive qualities—and, having found them, to celebrate.

The move from the familiar into the new style of encounter is an act of faith. The pastor or other leader will do well to remind himself often that between Egypt and the promised land, Moses and his flock spent more than a few hours in the wilderness. An honest group leader will readily admit to moments when he too pleads, "Oh, my Lord, send, I pray, some other person." (Exodus 4:13) However, we also need to remember that while they wandered around, not altogether sure what was happening or where they were going, the children of Israel became a nation and found God. The lasting results of their experience probably would not have happened had they taken the nearest freeway to the land of milk and honey.

Suffice it to say that the encounter group leader *initiates* a process. He guides his flock into the kinds of interaction that make it possible for them to open up to each other and to God.

Along the way, most participants will, at some time, find themselves in a painful wilderness. Self-discovery can seem devastating, and God can seem a long way off. Nonetheless, it is precisely in the struggle with this wilderness experience that one begins to find the way to wholeness. The group becomes a community of persons, with the wilderness as a common experience. In their new understanding and acceptance of each other comes a new understanding and acceptance of God.

Surprisingly (or is it?), the importance of relationships has been demonstrated many times previously in the church. One notable example is the Wesleyan revival in England in the eighteenth century. In his outstanding study *The Key To Change*, Dr. Gloster Udy of Australia demonstrates that the key to John Wesley's impact on English culture was the "class meeting." Its structure contained many similarities to modern encounter groups. For example, a disciple of the class meeting tried to form a group in his hometown. He printed a list of the specific values which would result from such a fellowship:

(1) Because we are ignorant and shortsighted, God reveals to one what is good for another. In the multitude of counselors there is wisdom.

(2) Because we are lovers of ourselves, we need friends who will show us our faults.

(3) Because we are weak and irresolute, we need a band of friends who are like-minded to inspire us with courage and confidence.

(4) Because we are lukewarm in religious duties, a holy fellowship will rekindle and keep alive the holy fervour.

119

That is the witness to the power of encounter in 1735! The class meeting provided a new "family" for broken persons, where, in the fresh air of caring relationships, they found God and new life. But when Methodism became a middle-class church, Methodists became self-righteous and no longer had the desire to share feelings and sins with each other. Coincidentally, the class meeting faded into oblivion.

Today, because the hollowness of being self-righteous and the loneliness of separation have become unbearable for many persons, God is once again calling people into a special fellowship, geared to the needs of this age. The signs of his presence are visible to any who have the eyes to see.

John the Baptist sent his followers to Jesus to ask, "Are you the One?" His answer was simply, "Go tell John what you hear and see." That is the intent of this book: to tell what we have seen and heard of the power of God in encounter groups. Summed up into one sentence, it is this: people are being changed in a predictable pattern that leads from brokenness and estrangement to wholeness.

What is this pattern? In his autobiography, *A Song of Ascents*, Dr. E. Stanley Jones described the elements of change in his own life which accompanied his conversion experience:

—a sense of forgiveness
—a sense of belonging
—a sense of purpose and direction
—a sense of not being alone
—a sense of being a person
—a sense of wholeness
—a sense of grace.

The discovery of these qualities produced one of the world's most remarkable personalities. Added together, they equal conversion—the most radical reformation of all.

Interestingly, Dr. Jones knew the rhetoric of the church for years before this personal change occurred. The change came in relationship to two persons whose *teachings* he scarcely mentions. Of evangelist Robert Bateman he says, ". . . through his rough exterior I saw reality within . . ." His other reference is to ". . . my beloved teacher, Miss Nellie Logan. . . ." What Stanley Jones discovered through Robert Bateman and Nellie Logan, others are now finding in the encounter group experience. There, every member is an evangelist to every other member.

In the open sharing of common failures and feelings, a member's first reaction often is, "Oh, I thought I was the only one who felt like that." The sense of belonging that results from such sharing is the strong glue that binds the group together. Forgiveness, too, plays a major role in group experience. Many persons find that learning to give and receive forgiveness is the key to new life. The one who knows that he belongs in a group of people who are forgiving of his humanness soon discovers that he is truly a real person.

All of these actions convey the most fundamental truths of the gospel. All of them point the way to wholeness. A person sits in a group week after week, hearing others say to him, "I hear you," "I love you," "I forgive you." It isn't far from there to understanding "God hears you," "God loves you," "God forgives you." We really shouldn't expect it to happen any other way. After all, God spoke to man for centuries, but his voice fell on deaf ears and half-understanding minds. Only when the Word became flesh did eyes open and a new relationship form between God and his people; love was only an idea until Love walked on the earth, touching people, living with them, weeping with them. Then love became a fact and a possibility.

Nothing less is true now. For example, grace is both the most needed and most rare experience we have. Grace is only an idea until grace comes alive for us in another person. Within the encounter group, grace comes in the privilege of not opening one's self. There are no invasions, no peeling of tender feelings. We learn the taste and feel of grace in such a simple way as that. Once the feeling is known, we discover that there is a lot more grace flowing between people than we realized. Other persons accept us far more than we know, because they know us far better than we think they do.

When a person discovers that a group of virtual strangers (although part of the same church "fellowship") can see through a mask which has been used for years—see the real person and accept that person—he knows the truth of saying, *O Lord, thou hast searched me and known me!* (Psalm 139:1) Every person who enters the arena of honesty and transparency is living out the high prayer (verses 23-24) of that same Psalm:

> *Search me, O God, and know my*
> *heart!*
> *Try me and know my thoughts!*
> *And see if there be any wicked*
> *way in me,*
> *and lead me in the way ever-*
> *lasting!*

The answer to the prayer is the rock-strewn path to wholeness. Amen, Lord. Let it be!

Appendixes

Appendix 1

□

Group Games

A group of married couples began their encounter following the pattern suggested in chapter 9. After the first several sessions, very few sensitivity games were used. The members of the group continued to interact in an open manner, facilitated by the leader and using the feedback technique.

Another group of married couples was not so spontaneous; they felt the need for something to "prime the pump." As persons who worked in creative and professional vocations, they felt secure in agreeing to take turns bringing in games. Each week the session began this way, with a different person facilitating an encounter experience.

Members in this second group frequently created their own techniques. This group however, tended to play it very safe. The leader often interceded to enable the group to use the game more meaningfully. At times, nothing really "happened"; the person leading just never got the game off the ground. That experience then became the point of encounter. How did he or she feel about the failure? How did the group feel? Were they able to relate creatively to each other in this situation?

Yet another group needed the leader to begin with a sensitivity game every week. They were single young adults, very inhibited, afraid of all relationships that went beyond the surface. A planned game was used during every session for six months. Often, the game was simple and short, sometimes involving physical touch—a most threatening experience for this particular group. A few minutes of such programmed activity provided enough content to carry through the entire session.

Notice that *these games are not mere parlor pastimes.* They are used sparingly and for a specific purpose. You probably will need only one for any ninety-minute session. You may, however, need to "pull one out of the hat" in the midst of the session, either to enable some member to dramatize his unexpressed feelings or to move the group interaction to a deeper level. The main thing to realize here is that we do not use games just to play. The emphasis is on exploring and developing personal relationships.

In chapter 8 we took the term "game" out of its destructive or flippant connotation and defined it as a technique which (1) helps persons to dramatize their internal feelings, or (2) facilitates interaction around a person's need for inclusion, control, or affection. An expanded awareness of one's self, of others, or of one's self in relationship to others often requires the acting out of that relationship.

This appendix offers a basic package of some of these games. After you are experienced, you may want to innovate your own and to develop variations on a theme to fit the need of the hour. Many of these games are far removed from their source. One of the phenomena of the encounter movement is the swapping of game techniques whenever leaders get together. We make no claim on these few we share here. Use them, adapt them, reproduce them, share them.

There are several excellent collections to which you may wish to refer. (See the bibliography for more details on these aids.) Pfeiffer and Jones' *A Handbook of Structured Experiences for Human Relations Training* contains seventy-four games of wide variety. Lyman Coleman's exciting series of "mini courses" in self-discovery are Christian in orientation and suggest many techniques, including those aimed at Bible study. *Joy: Expanding Human Awareness* by William Schutz is a primary textbook containing many games which can be adapted to your purposes. Daniel Malamud and Solomon Machover's *Toward Self-Understanding* is an extensive collection of experiments used in a therapy group setting. *Sense Relaxation Below Your Mind* by Bernard Gunther illustrates and instructs in specific sensitivity exercises involving bodily contact with one's self, with the group, and between married couples.

If you, as a leader, feel uncomfortable with games which involve touch or physical contact, please don't think you must do these. When the leader is "uptight" about a technique, his anxiety will come across to the group. It will be helpful for you and for the group if you can share these fears, as well as your own insecurity in your position as leader. Others will then understand why they are feeling uneasy, and you can all deal with the situation honestly. Such sharing, in turn, will lower the anxiety level for everyone. Whatever follows will be more genuine and creative.

A basic anthology of games for encounter groups

1. Bible passage paraphrase

Goals: To share a scripture passage with others at a deeply personal level. To enable each person to find the passage's relevance for his life. To explore new depths of awareness of self, others, and God with the help of the Bible.

Materials: A Bible, paper, and pencil for each person.

Process: (1) Assign one passage and have everyone take ten minutes to read it, then translate it into his own words, using few or none of the words from the text.

(2) Next, gather in triads (subgroups of three) and share the new versions, discussing the differences in personal meanings.

(3) After about fifteen minutes, have each individual write on his paper how he would live differently if he took his translation with absolute seriousness.

(4) Regather in the triads and share these insights together.

(5) Finally, have the entire group discuss in the circle how they feel about this exercise.

2. Bible role

Goal: To allow each participant to understand more deeply a passage of scripture and its application to his life.

Materials: A Bible for each person.

Process: (1) Have everyone meditate on the same passage of scripture, preferably one in which a number of different characters participate.

(2) For fifteen minutes read it again and again. Say to the group: "Put yourself into the situation. Go over it enough times to filter *out* the sense of who you *want* to be, and instead find out who you *are* in the story. With which character do you identify? Feel the part. What is happening to you in the situation?"

(3) Now go around the group and have each person share who he is in that passage and why.

3. The big question

Goal: To cause each person to think more deeply about the meaning of life.

Process: (1) Divide the group into dyads, pairing persons who know each other the least. Sitting knee to knee, one is to ask the other, "Who are you?" He may make no other comment. No matter what his partner says, he only repeats the question. The partner will attempt to answer the question each time it is asked, *without repeating himself*.

(2) After several minutes, have them change roles. This time let the question be, "What do you want?"

(3) Afterwards, have the group talk about the experience.

4. Brainstorming your personality

Goal: For each participant to discover more about himself and how he comes across to others.

Materials: Newsprint (on wall or easel), plus felt pen or crayon.

Process: (1) In volunteer order, let members in succession stand at the easel. The group is to brainstorm all the words they can think of to describe the subject person, who writes these descriptive words on the newsprint as they are offered. The words are called out rapidly. (Note: the key here is the word "descriptive." This is not an evaluation event. The anticipated result should be a strong affirmation, but the concept of feedback should guide all responses.)

(2) When the group runs out of words, tear off the newsprint and post it to the side. Now, using all the words, the group is to compose a paragraph about the subject, who continues to write (without responding) what the group dictates. After the paragraph is complete, the subject may ask questions for clarification.

(3) When each member of the group has had a turn, have the group talk about how they feel and what they learned.

5. Breaking in

Goals: To acknowledge the fear of being excluded. To act out the need to be accepted. To experience the fact of acceptance as one of the group.

Caution: Can be rough activity, so sharp furniture should be removed. Most people will not get too rough, but if someone should, let that be part of the feedback. Obviously, persons with some physical disability or limitation should either use caution or not participate.

Process: The group stands in a circle, interlocking arms. One (perhaps a member who really feels he's on the outside) is left out of the tight circle and is ignored. The outsider tries to break in wherever and however he can. The group tries to keep him out. When he gets in, the group embraces him. (This may be repeated for all members of the group.) At the conclusion, have group members discuss how they felt about the process.

6. Creative conflict

Goal: To discover that anger is acceptable and can be creative—that it does not mean "I hate you."

Process: This role play is described for a group of married couples, but can be adapted for others.

(1) Ask for two volunteers, not married to each other, male and female. Assign them the following situation.

He: "You worked hard all day, with many demands on your time and people on your back. You look forward to coming home and just relaxing, not having to think about anything. After dinner you head for your favorite chair and the TV—there is an old movie on that you've missed and always wanted to see."

She: "You have been home all day with the kids and are exhausted (or you've been at your job all day). The kids monopolized the conversation at dinner and now that the meal is over, your husband has disappeared. After cleaning the kitchen, you come in to your husband. All day you have looked forward to this hour and have stored up things to discuss. You find him glued to the TV. You start the conversation; he shushes you because the movie is starting."

Take the play from there.

(2) When the action has been going for a while, substitute the other's real spouse for one of the actors and have them continue the play. Note any changes in tone or approach.

(3) Have the entire group discuss how they feel about what happened. Raise questions such as "Does anger mean 'I don't love you'? Do you avoid conflict in your marriage? Is conflict creative? Do you state your feelings in terms of what is happening to you, or do you state them in terms of what is wrong with the other person?"

7. Earliest memory

Goals: To enable married couples to share something new. To discover how well each partner listens and is present with his or her spouse.

Process: (1) In a group of married couples (can be adapted to unmarried groups), have participants close their eyes, relax (perhaps lie down), and think back to the very first thing they can remember. Allow several minutes for this.

(2) Then have spouses face each other, knee to knee (dyads), and share with each other in full detail this earliest memory.

(3) Now have two couples form into a group of four. Each person is to tell the other couple, without assistance or interference, his or her spouse's earliest memory. The report is to remain uncorrected.

(4) Finally, have the group return to the larger circle and talk about what each person learned or felt in this exercise. Ask such questions as—"Did you talk but not listen? Was it hard to recover early memories? Did you and your spouse find similarities? Did you learn anything new?"

8. Fish bowl

Goals: For each person to learn more about how he comes across to others and how he relates to group process. To discover how observing he is of the behavior of others and how open he can be in sharing with another what he observed about himself.

Process: See appendix 2—week 3.

Variations: See *What is the church?*—an exercise found at the end of this appendix.

9. Fulfillment in marriage

Goals: To enable married couples to face realistically the marriage relationship and to discover how well they are communicating with each other.

Process: (1) Divide the group of married couples into two subgroups so that spouses are not together. If there is an auxiliary room, use it for one subgroup, or else put the subgroups in corners.

(2) In each subgroup, members are, in turn, to answer the question "Where is the greatest satisfaction and fulfillment in your marriage?" The group is to accept what each person says without comment, asking questions only for clarification.

(3) Now repeat the process with this question—"Where is the greatest lack of fulfillment and satisfaction in your marriage?"

(4) Bring the entire group together, with spouses sitting next to each other. Go around the group, each person speaking for his or her spouse, and saying, "She (he) would say the greatest satisfaction and fulfillment in our marriage is _____. The greatest lack is _____."

(5) Go around again, this time sharing, "Did your spouse say about the same thing you have said?"

(6) Have the total group talk about how they feel.

10. Gift giving

Goals: To have each person affirmed by the other members of the group. To enjoy the blessing of giving something to others.

Materials: Pencils and paper.

Process: (1) Have each person write a list of "seven things you *do not* like about yourself." Have them hold up their hands when finished, with the leader timing how long it takes.

(2) Now have each person list "seven things you *do* like about yourself." Time this. Usually, the second list takes much longer, which means persons are weak in their feelings of self-worth. Have the group discuss how they feel about these two lists.

(3) Say to the group: "To help us feel more affirmed, we will give gifts to each other. Silently list all the persons in the group, and opposite their name put a gift you would like to give them, something personal just for that individual."

(4) Now, have the members, in turn, go out of the room. While each is out, go around the group and have each one tell what he gave the one who is absent. A secretary will prepare a list of the gifts addressed to the one member. Do not identify who gave what gift. Repeat this step for each group member, the secretary holding all the master lists.

(5) After everyone has been out and returned, give one member the list of his gifts. Have him read it aloud, express his feelings, and ask questions for clarification if he wishes. Repeat in turn for each member of the group.

(6) Invite members to take home the list of gifts given to them, and the list of gifts they gave the others. These can be used daily as members pray for each other for one week.

11. Group fantasy

Goals: To deepen the common, shared experiences of the group. To discover hitherto unrealized relationships among group members. To increase awareness of self and others.

Process: (1) From the group as a whole choose three or four persons and ask them to lie on the floor with their heads touching at the center and forming the hub of a wheel, their bodies forming the spokes. Ask them and the other group members sitting around the circle to close their eyes. Everyone is to relax and rest.

(2) Only those lying on the floor may speak. One begins by telling whatever picture comes to his imagination. All others will follow in their imaginations, picturing whatever is described. Those on the floor will enter the fantasy and add to it whatever is going on in their heads. There should be no deliberate attempts to make up a continuing story. Let each person's fantasy roam free and undirected, with everyone in the room picturing whatever is being described. Those lying on the floor may speak and give their input to the fantasy.

(3) When someone else wants to enter verbally, he must first get down on the floor and become another spoke in the wheel. If someone is finished speaking and wishes to with-

draw, he gets up from the floor and goes back to his place, on the rim of the circle, meanwhile continuing silent participation in the fantasy.

(4) The game ends when everyone gets up, or when the group agrees it's over. The leader may wish to wind it up at a high point. Most of the group will probably have had a very moving experience, the details of which will be as vivid as if they had literally lived it out together.

(5) After a few moments of silent reflection, have the group discuss their feelings. Clarify the relationships, the feelings of affection and hostility, and the significance of what went on in the fantasy.

12. Hands in a pile

Goals: To experience unity in the group. To act out a group benediction.

Process: See appendix 2—week 1.

13. House building

Goals: For each participant to discover how much about himself he has communicated nonverbally to the others. To discover that others know him better than he imagined, even after only short contact, and that they accept him as he is. To learn he can trust his impressions.

Materials: A watch for time-keeping.

Process: See chapter 9.

14. If I could not fail

Goals: For each participant to discover some of his fears, to share some of his dreams, and to understand better the others in the group.

Process: (1) Ask the group to think in silence about this question: "If I knew I could not fail, what is one thing I would like to do in my life?"

(2) After a few minutes of meditation, go around the group and invite each person to share honestly his thoughts on this question. Then go around the group a second time

and invite each member to affirm and support another. For example, "Mary, I feel I want to help you achieve your goal." Or, "Joe, I am going to pray for you each day that you might get to do (the thing you wish)."

15. If you were a . . .

Goals: To discover how the members of the group feel about each other and how they "come across." To learn how to receive and accept honest criticism, as well as how to give it.

Process: The group focuses on each member in turn, going around the circle and stating for the subject, "If you were an animal, you would be a (chipmunk, beaver, mule, lion, etc.)." Do not make additional or explanatory comments, but after each round invite the subject to ask clarifying questions if he wishes. After each person has been the subject, invite group discussion—"How did you feel about this? What did you learn?"

Variation: Instead of animals, use foods or colors.

16. In case of fire

Goals: For each participant to discover his real values, to express his care for others in the group, and to receive the feelings of others for him.

Materials: Paper and pencil for each member.

Process: (1) Each person is to list the first ten things he would grab and take out of his house if it should catch fire.

(2) Rate them in order of priority, one to ten.

(3) Each is to take the first five priorities on his list and write opposite them why they are valuable to him.

(4) Ask each person to share with the group his five things and why they are of value.

(5) Go around the group a second time with this question: "If you had to give these five things away, to which person in the group would you give each one and why?"

17. Instant encounter

Goals: For each participant to discover his own reactions

in a nonverbal encounter with another person—how honest or dishonest he is in expressing his feelings—how difficult or easy it is to encounter another.

Process: (1) Have the group divide, half lining up across one wall and facing the other half lined against the opposite wall. Have each person identify his or her partner (exact opposite) in the other line. Have partners fix their eyes on each other, remain silent, and begin to walk very slowly toward each other, never diverting their eyes. During the instructions, tell them they are not to plan what to do when they meet. As they draw near, they are to do whatever they feel inwardly impelled to do. They may continue the encounter, without words, as long as they wish.

(2) After the encounter, have the partners sit down knee-to-knee and discuss the experience. How did they feel about it? Uncomfortable? Excited? Did they repress their real impulses?

(3) Now have the entire group talk about the experience.

18. Lift every body

Goals: To enable each person to discover his feelings about tenderness and about his relationship to each other in the group.

Process: (1) Half of the group members lie on the floor on their backs, closing their eyes and taking a few moments to breathe deeply and relax. The other members of the group go from person to person, gently picking up different heads, arms, legs, hands, hips. The persons being lifted are to remain completely passive. Those doing the lifting are to move the part being lifted, weigh it, feel it, note whether they are getting help or resistance from each person.

(2) After five minutes of this moving about and lifting, have the two groups change places and repeat the process.

(3) During the discussion about how everyone felt, note feelings of fear, mistrust, or joy, and the differences in how members related to one or another. Were some rough, some timorous, some compassionate?

(4) The leader may wish to observe who was ill at ease, who was gentle, who was silly, etc., and feed this back into the discussion.

19. Moments of peak experience

Goals: For each participant to discover that the moments of highest joy and unity are those in which something is being communicated to him. To help him be aware of his peak experiences.

Materials: Pencil and paper for each member.

Process: (1) Have each person divide his paper into two columns. In the first, list those moments which were peak experiences in joy, clarity, one-person unity. In the column opposite, note what it was that induced such strong feeling and made it a peak experience. Repeat the process for the "bottom" experiences of life.

(2) Now have the group share some of their feelings and discoveries with each other. Ask what makes them feel most alive and inspired.

20. Nonverbal communication

Goals: To experience the closeness with another person that is so often blocked by words. To discover how much is communicated by touch, by look, and by feeling—those "vibrations" which are often obscured by speaking. To discover the feeling of being close to another person.

Process: See chapter 9.

21. Nonverbal affirmation circle

Goal: To practice giving and receiving feelings of affirmation and affection.

Process: (1) Have each member of the group, in turn, sit in the center, eyes closed or blindfolded, while the other members take turns coming forward and, without any words, affirming the subject. The subject is not to respond, but to remain inactive. He is only to receive, not give.

(2) After all have had a turn, have the group talk about how they feel.

137

22. Nonverbal rejection

Goal: To deal with feelings of rejection.

Process: (1) Have the group mill about the room silently until they form into threes (triads). Now instruct them to re-form into twos (dyads). To achieve this, the three are to decide nonverbally which of them is to leave. The "spares" then form into groups of twos.

(2) Now have the group sit in a circle and share how they felt about this process. (Note: this exercise should not be used with persons who seem to conceive of themselves as outcasts or "not OK.")

23. Passing in the circle

Goals: To enable each participant to express caring (or lack of it) for individuals in the group. To discover his ability, or inability, to trust others. To experience the joy of being cared for by the group. To feel accepted.

Process: See chapter 9.

24. Personal crest

Goals: For each participant to gain new insight about himself in relationship to others, God, world, self, goals. To explore two phases of Christian love: caring and sharing (listening, being present with another, giving, opening up to another).

Process: See appendix 2—week 1.

25. Experiment in prayer

Goals: To understand better the vitality of intercessory prayer. To draw the group together around a specific prayer experience. To become aware of feelings about prayer.

Materials: A rough, natural rock; a growing plant; a stool or stand.

Process: The group is seated in a circle with an empty stool or chair in the center. The leader participates as one of the group.

(1) *Inanimate object.* After instructing the group, place a

rock (preferably in its original state) on the empty seat. Give the group no instruction other than something like this: "Here is our first object of prayer. Bow your head, close your eyes, and pray, silently or aloud, for the rock." Allow about one minute. The leader ends the prayer time with a simple "amen" and immediately asks, "How did you feel about that?" (The same invitation to pray silently or aloud is given for each object to follow, and always the group is asked to express their feelings.)

(2) *Growing plant.* Place some plant that is growing (not cut flowers) on the empty seat and repeat instructions.

(3) *Unknown generalized group.* Suggest prayer for some large group of people who are unknown as persons to the group. Examples are those in prison or the mentally ill.

(4) *Unknown* (personally) *individual.* Tell the group to picture someone who is (1) personally unknown and (b) not present or near and to pray for that person. Example—the president.

(5) *Known person, not present.* The group is, as individuals, to picture in the empty seat some close friend or relative who is not present and to pray for that person.

(6) *Known person, present.* One of the group is to sit in the seat. The person can be selected or be a volunteer. After the time of prayer (which can be a little longer than a minute), ask the person who was prayed for to express his feelings. Then invite observations from the others.

(7) *Known person, present, hands touching.* Using the same person as in No. 6, have the group gather around and place their hands on the person as they pray. Once more, let the person who is prayed for be the first to express his feeling.

(8) *Encounter prayer (optional).* Select two persons from the group who seem to be responding strongly and positively to the experiment. One of them should be someone who is able to express himself (herself) well in a group. Have these two persons sit in the center and face one another, hands joined. The group is to gather around and concentrate on

looking at the two in the center. The one who is able to express himself most easily is asked to pray for the other person, *eyes open and looking at that person.* The pray-er will close his own prayer. The two in the center are asked to give feedback, first about the experience, then about the group.

(9) Have the group discuss the total prayer experience. The leader should listen for and reflect any significant feelings or new insights expressed.

26. Questions for sharing yourself

Goals: To enable a group to know each other more quickly and at a deeper level. To enable persons to know themselves more deeply through questions not usually thought about.

Materials: Pencils and paper (optional).

Process: Have group members think about the following questions and then share their thoughts verbally with the group.

a) "Where would you live if you had your choice, and what would you do there?"

b) "Who is the most important person in your life, and why?"

c) "If you could have ten minutes with Jesus, what two things would you ask him?"

d) "What suffering have you known, and what effect has it had on you?"

e) "What keeps you from being the person you want to be?"

f) "What is the most significant thing that has happened to you in the last three years?"

g) "Tell five good things about yourself."

27. Role playing

Goals: May be used in a wide variety of situations to act out feelings of affection, control, or inclusion among group members. May be used to help members find new insight or solutions to specific problems.

Process: (1) When a situation arises which needs to be clarified or helped through to some resolution, suggest a role play and ask the group to define the issue—for example, a conflict between two members (or a person present and some other person not of the group).

(2) Select the players (or ask for volunteers) to interact with the principal person; assign the roles; set the scene or situation. Have them proceed to act out the play, in their natural or assumed role, as the situation dictates.

(3) After a few minutes, cut the action (when there has been enough to project the outcome, or an impasse is reached, or it naturally concludes). Ask the *players* to report their feelings and insights. Then ask the *group* to feed back their feelings and insights.

Variations: (a) Involve the total group (or subgroups) in the action, leaving no audience.

(b) Assign an extra player to stand near each role player and be his alter ego—voicing private thoughts, feelings, unconscious motives.

(c) Stop the action midway and replace one or more actors with other members of the group. Who will then bring their own reactions into play.

(d) It may be helpful to replay the situation with changes suggested by the discussion, or even with a new cast.

28. Self-image poster
Goals: For each member to discover how he sees himself. To reveal to others how he sees himself. To discover he can be accepted as he is.

Materials: Magazines with plenty of pictures and advertisements. Scissors for each participant; paste or glue; wastebaskets. Optional: quiet background music.

Process: See chapter 9.

29. Self-knowledge inventory
Goals: To understand feelings and responses. To enable group members to know each other on a more personal level.

Materials: Paper and pencils.

Process: (1) Form dyads. Dictate one of the unfinished statements from the following list, and have each person complete it for himself.

(2) Ask each person to share his answer with his partner, after which they will talk about their feelings and responses.

(3) Have the partners switch and repeat the process, using another statement from the list. Go on with as many different combinations of partners as time permits. Allow sufficient time at the end to have the entire group discuss their own feelings and awareness of each other.

"When I enter a new group, I feel _____."
"When people first meet me, they _____."
"When people remain silent, I feel _____."
"When someone does all the talking, I _____."
"I feel annoyed when the leader _____."
"In a group, I am most afraid of _____."
"When someone feels hurt, I _____."
"Those who really know me think I am _____."
"I feel closest to others when _____."
"People like me when I _____."
"I feel loved most when _____."
"I could be _____."
"I am _____."

30. Strength bombardment

Goals: To appreciate the good in group members. To become more aware of how the members of the group see each other. To learn which strengths are showing and which are not.

Process: In turn, each member of the group is silent while the others concentrate on him, bombarding him verbally with all the things they like about him and see as strengths. Do this in a brainstorming manner and keep up the bombardment until the group runs out of words. Then move on to the next person. After everyone has had a turn, let each share how he felt.

31. Three-dimensional triad—no. 1

Goal: To become aware of the dimensions of Christian love and how each person is able to experience them.

Process: (1) Explain to the group that Christian love has these aspects:

"*I care*," which requires focusing attention on the other person, appreciating him, denying self the spotlight to give it to another.

"*I give*," which requires a person to express himself, to give up his privacy, to invite the other person into his life.

"*I learn*," which requires a person to deal with himself and the other person in relationships, and to be open to truth about himself, the other person, and their expectations of each other.

(2) Begin by dividing into triads and have the subgroup members number from one to three. Be sure husband and wife are not in the same triad.

(3) Assign a role to each number: No. 1—"I give"; No. 2—"I care"; No. 3—"I learn." Now, for five minutes No. 1 will share with No. 2 out of his heart on "expectations I have of my closest friend." No. 2 will listen, be present, draw out, care. No. 3 will silently observe the behavior and feelings of the other two.

(4) After five minutes, stop all the triads. Have No. 3 feed back to No. 1 and No. 2 how well they performed their roles and any discoveries he made during the conversation.

(5) Now rotate the roles and repeat the process.

(6) Rotate again and repeat until each person has played all three roles.

(7) At the end, have the whole group sit together and report on how they did and what difficulties they had.

Variation: Have as the discussion topic, "expectations I have of my spouse." Afterward, have couples sit knee-to-knee and talk about their expectations of each other in marriage.

32. Three-dimensional triad—no. 2

Goal: To discover that negative feelings do not have to be destructive when they are acknowledged and given the context of self-disclosure rather than hostile attack on another person.

Process: (1) Divide the group into triads and describe the dimensions of Christian love as outlined in "Three-Dimensional Triad No. 1."

(2) Have each person take a role: "care," "share," "learn." Let the "share" person talk about "hateful feelings I have had toward my father and mother." The "caring" person draws him out. The "learning" person listens to the speaker for specific descriptions of behavior that angers him. Also, is the speaker stating his bad feelings in terms of what is happening to him rather than attacking the parents?

(3) After a few minutes, let the "learning" person feed back to the other two what he observed.

(4) Then rotate the roles.

(5) When everyone has played all three roles using this same topic, let the total group regather and share how they felt about this. What did they discover about negative feelings? Do negative feelings mean a lack of love?

Variation: In a group of married couples, follow this discussion of negative feelings with dyads of spouses sitting knee-to-knee and sharing with each other "things you do that make you hard to live with."

33. Trust lift

Goals: To experience the tender care of the group for individual members. To discover how much each participant trusts the group.

Process: (1) Have the subject (a volunteer) lie on his back on the floor, eyes closed and relaxed. The group gathers around him, slipping their hands under his body all around. Be sure all extremities are supported. Now lift him slowly and gently to waist level. With many hands, he will seem surprisingly light, so take care not to go too fast. Now gently rock him back and forth. Then continue the lift, ever so slowly, pausing at shoulder level, and then on up above the heads of the group.

(2) Reverse this process, slowly lowering the person in stages, finally laying him back on the floor so gently he hardly knows he is down. While he rests, the group slowly backs away.

(3) Now let him share his feelings and the group share theirs. Repeat with other members if desired.

34. Trust walk

Goals: To discover to what extent participants can trust each other. To experience the joy of caring for another person and of being cared for.

Process: See appendix 2—week 3.

Variation: A person with eyes closed moves on his own without being led. His partner cares for him by seeing that he does not injure himself and helps him explore his environment.

35. What is the church?

Goals: For each participant to learn about himself in group interaction. To discover his feelings about the church. (Note: This is similar to the Fish Bowl.)

Materials: Magazines, scissors, glue, construction paper.

Process: (1) Form into two equal groups. Assign each person to a partner in the other subgroup. Have one subgroup sit around the materials and prepare a group montage which illustrates symbolically the answer to the question "What is the church?" Those working on the montage will discuss the question, choose the symbols from the magazines, and develop a picture which expresses their group feeling about the church.

(2) The members of the other subgroup will stand around the outside of the inner circle, each person observing the group at work and especially observing the behavior of his partner in relationship to the others.

(3) After the montage is complete, have the partners from the two subgroups meet in dyads (twos), the observer telling the participant what he observed and how he felt during the process.

(4) Now reverse the roles of the subgroups and repeat the process.

(5) Afterwards, have the entire group talk about their feelings and what they learned.

Appendix 2

□

An Encounter Workshop

We suggested that one way to initiate groups in the church is to announce a series of three encounter workshops to be held on three successive weeks. In this appendix we want to offer some guidelines for leading these workshops effectively. These are some of the procedures we tried that worked well for us.

WEEK 1:

When those responding arrive, give them name tags and have them sit in one large circle. Have each person tell his name and answer some specific personal question, such as "Where would you live if you could, and what would you do there?"

Give a short summary of what an encounter group is all about. Though you will want to make up your own outline of basic points, here are some important thoughts recapitulated.

"Everything we do in the group is based on the assumption that God intends our lives to be made up of good things (that is, the 'abundant life'). These things are listed in Galatians 5:22–23. (Review them. Note that these are the fruits of the Holy Spirit, and they all involve relationships.)

"Relationships with self, others, and God are of primary importance. However, all relationships have two dimensions. They have an agony and an ecstasy, and you can't be sensitive to one without being sensitive to the other. For example, because we are afraid of the pain of being rejected, we do not risk deep relationships. The result is that we become isolated, and the pain of isolation is as bad as the pain of rejection. We might as well risk. If we would know the joy of relationship, we must also risk the pain of rejection. To find the gifts of love, joy, peace, etc., we must become involved with others. This is why we are here.

"Another way to state the purpose of the encounter group is 'awareness.' (Ask these questions slowly, thoughtfully.)

"*Self-awareness*: How do you feel right now about this moment? What are your needs, your weaknesses, your vulnerable places, your strengths and securities? Where do you want to change and grow?

"*Other-awareness*: How do the persons around you feel? What are they saying to you nonverbally? Will you learn to trust your inner feelings, to see with a third eye, to perceive with a sixth sense? Do you recognize your feelings about these people? Why do you feel as you do? Will you build a community of trust with them?

"*God-awareness*: When you become *self*-aware and *other*-aware, God is able to break through 'into the midst' of those relationships. Review Acts 1 and 2; recall who was there and the former conflicts between them. Was what went on in the Upper Room the first Christian encounter group? Was Pentecost the result?

"How do we achieve all this in a group? We do not study books or bring in outside material. The focus of our attention is each other. We study the relationships in the group. The encounter itself becomes our resource material.

"We will use some simple techniques. For example, we will stay at a feeling level. We will not deal with ideas or issues apart from the relationships in the group. We will play certain kinds of 'games' to dramatize our feelings. (Illustrate this.) We will use a way of communicating with each other called 'feedback.' (See chapter 8.) This helps each person to know himself and at the same time enables him to be real and open with others. (Illustrate this.)"

At the close of your summary invite questions for clarification.

Now have the group mill about the room (see chapter 9— session 3) and form dyads. Distribute paper and pencils and ask each person to draw a personal coat-of-arms. Each can draw a rough shield and divide it into four quadrants.

Say to the groups, "In each of the four areas draw a symbol which represents how you feel about your relationship to God, your family, your work, and the community. Thus, you have four sections on your coat-of-arms, each carrying some symbol or picture of a different relationship in your life. Underneath the shield write a word or a motto which sums up where you are now in your life."

These crests should be simply made. Allow about ten minutes for the exercise, then have the two partners sit knee-to-knee and let each explain his crest to the other. You may suggest that two aspects of Christian love are caring and sharing and that each person will have the opportunity to give himself to the other in the meaning of his symbolic crest. Then he will be able to care for the other in listening to his partner.

After this exchange is complete, have the papers put out of sight and ask each dyad to move together with another dyad. In this new grouping of four, ask each person to introduce his partner to the other two persons, drawing from all the things learned about the other in the sharing time. The person being introduced will remain quiet, neither correcting nor adding to the words of the partner. After all four have been introduced to each other, have them discuss how they felt about the process. How well did the partner introduce them? How well had he listened and been present with them? What did each learn about himself, his relationships, and his ability to be truly present with another person?

Now have the groups of four stand and lock arms. Without talking, they are to mill about the room in fours until they feel a consensus about a comfortable place to stop. When all have stopped milling, ask each group of four to pick another group, so that they become eight. This group will be together for the rest of the workshop series. Have them sit down and talk over how they feel about being together and why they chose each other. Ask each group to give themselves a name. Pass a sheet around each circle to record who is in which group.

You are coming to the end of the first workshop session. (Before closing, emphasize to the group the desirability of wearing casual clothes to the remaining sessions. Ideally, this matter should be brought up when the workshops are being announced so that persons will wear casual clothes to the first session.) As a benediction, have everyone stand in their group circles, close their eyes, and pile one hand on top of the other in the center. Pause to experience the closeness of the group. With eyes still closed, slowly raise the pile of hands together to shoulder level. Pause. Lower them to waist level. Now reach down as far as they will go without separating, then up as high as they can reach, and back to the center. Slowly slide the hands out, one by one, being aware of each other all the time. Then the participants can open their eyes. The session is adjourned.

WEEK 2:

As the group assembles, have them gather in their smaller units. Have any new persons sit in the middle; ask them how they feel about their situation. Ask the other groups how they feel about the new people. What do they want to do about the situation?

If there is no agreement on how to integrate these new

people into the existing groups, have them try to "break in."
Each group stands in a tight circle with arms locked together,
backs to the outside. The newcomers mill about and try
physically to break into the group they choose. The group
tries to keep them out; they try harder to force their way in.
Either they break in, or fast-talk their way in, or perhaps the
group will open to them. (Don't suggest these options. Let it
be spontaneous.) Once the newcomer is in, the group is to
express their acceptance of that person in some nonverbal
way. Now have the groups sit down and tell how they feel
about the experience.

Note that this way of integrating newcomers will be far
more effective than having them form their own group.
Having missed the first meeting, they will never feel at home
that way. Our experience is that most of them do not return
for the third week if forced to form a new group.

At this point, you might address everyone as they remain
in their groups, summarizing what went on last week. Say to
them: "Everything we do in these meetings calls forth feelings
from us. Feelings or emotions are not good or bad in themselves; rather, they are facts about ourselves. We need to learn
to be conscious of these feelings about ourselves, about
others, and about God. When we accept our feelings as facts,
then we can make decisions about whether we want to reinforce them or change our behavior and our attitudes. This is
freedom. Now we are acting rather than reacting. Now we are
responsible persons."

During the rest of this session, invite the groups to participate in house building, each group acting independently. (See
chapter 9—session 2.)

As the period closes, invite the group members to join
hands around their circle, look at each other for a minute,
then close their eyes and pray silently for each person in the
group. After a minute, ask them to stand and say goodnight
to each other nonverbally.

151

WEEK 3:

Ask each person, upon arriving, to go to his group. If some are new, follow the procedure used last week in having them integrate into the existing groups.

When all are settled down, explain that this time the group will learn how to receive and express nonverbal communication. Say something like: "So often words hide our real feelings and confuse our relationship with each other. Our faces, eyes, and body movements say one thing while our words say another, and the people around us are confused. Some nonverbal communication will stimulate our senses to greater awareness of ourselves and others. Remember, it is into the more genuine, accepting relationships that the Spirit of God can find best access."

Refer to chapter 9—session 3 for instructions on relaxing exercises and exploring a shoulder, feeling space, and non-verbal conversation between hands and then eyes (members within each group will pair off for this).

Now, using the same dyads, explain that they are to lead each other silently on a "trust walk." One will lead; the other will close his eyes and be led. For five minutes the walk will take place around the room, out into the building and yard, wherever you set the boundaries. After five minutes canvass the area, calling that it is time to change. The team members will reverse their roles. After another five minutes, call for everyone to return to the room. There, in the small groups, ask them to share their feelings. "Did you trust the other person? Did you prefer to lead or be led? Why? How did you decide who would lead first? Did you feel let down by your partner? Why?"

Next, each group will experiment with a *fish bowl*. In the dyads decide who shall be No. 1 and who No. 2. Have the "ones" form an inner circle, seated. The "twos" stand around the outside, across the circle where each can observe his partner. The inside group is going to hold a conversation. The outside partner is to note silently how the person he is observing acts with the group, what nonverbal language he uses, how the group itself gets started, who is involved, who avoids risks and stays out of trouble, who controls the group.

Now instruct the inside group that they are to discuss "the value of encounter groups." After ten minutes, stop the process. Ask the dyads (partners) to sit knee-to-knee while the "observer" tells the "talker" what he observed about his behavior, communication, and relationships. Also, the observer should share his own feelings about how he himself was responding to the events. After five minutes of this sharing, have the "ones" and "twos" reverse their roles and repeat the process. This time have the "twos" discuss "What is man's greatest need today?"

The last part of this session is called *the appreciation of bread and wine*. Explain that the group is going to expand their awareness and appreciation of some common things.

Place in the center of each group a small loaf of French bread and a clear glass of grape juice on a small table or upturned wastebasket. A white linen napkin or even a paper towel may be placed under the objects. Ask the group to sit quietly and study the loaf of bread with their eyes. Experience it; be present with it. One person may now reach out and take the loaf in hand. He will feel—weigh—smell— explore it while the others watch. Then he passes this precious loaf to the next person, and in doing so, looks into his eyes. Each in turn will feel, weigh, smell, and experience the loaf while the others watch. When it reaches the last person, ask him to hold it for further instructions.

Say something to this effect: "When Jesus took the loaf, he said, 'This is my Body which is given for you.' This may be important for you; it may not. Give it your own meaning while the person who now holds the loaf breaks it in two. Break it very, very slowly, a fraction of an inch at a time while the group watches closely. Identify with the loaf; feel it emotionally; experience it break."

Now that it is broken and one half returned to the table,

have the holder study the inside, break off a piece for himself, and hold his small piece while he passes the loaf on, looking into his neighbor's eyes. When the half has gone around and everyone holds a piece, place it with the other half.

Ask everyone to look at the cup of grape juice. Appreciate its rich color. Think of Jesus the night he passed the cup and said, "This is my blood of the covenant which is poured out for many for the forgiveness of sin." Let one person now take the cup and touch his piece of bread to the surface of the juice. Say to him: "Watch it soak in, mingling red with white. Quickly place it in your mouth, pass the cup to the next person, and close your eyes as you slowly chew the bread and wine mixture. Do not swallow until it is all liquefied in your mouth. Experience the taste, the odor, the feel, and remember Jesus."

When the cup completes the circle, put it back on the stand and ask everyone to open his eyes and look at the others in his group. When all the groups have finished, have them share a season of prayer within their circle. Invite all who will to lead in a sentence or two.

Before the group is dismissed, pass out return postcards on which they can check their desire to continue a weekly encounter group and what time would be best.

Annotated Bibliography

Blees, Robert. *Counseling With Teen-agers.* Philadelphia: Fortress Press, 1968.

Chapter 3, "Creative Use of Growth Groups," discusses the use of small groups with teen-agers, as well as the pastor's relationship with them. Several techniques or "games" described. Excellent.

Casteel, John, ed. *The Creative Role of Interpersonal Groups in the Church Today.* New York: Association Press, 1968.

Casteel sets today's personal group movement in historical perspective with the church of the first century, eighteenth-century England, and frontier America. Nine contributors trace the current renewal of the church through the rediscovery of small personal groups.

The Creative Role of Interpersonal Groups in the Church Today. New York: Association Press, 1968.

Follows the development of interpersonal groups in the 1960s. Specialized types of groups discussed include social action, prayer, therapy, counseling, occupation-centered, seminar, etc. Good discussion of the place of the group in today's world.

Chamberlain, David, and Chamberlain, Diane. *Marriage Enrichment Programs for Church Couples.* La Jolla, California: Love Training Associates, 1971.

Programmed instructions for leaders in helping an encounter group of married couples clarify love roles. Also includes a section (entitled "How Jesus Loves") applying current understanding of interpersonal relations to passages from the gospels.

155

Clinebell, Howard, Jr. *The Mental Health Ministry of the Local Church.* Nashville: Abingdon Press, 1972.

A challenging practical guidebook for making the church's ministry more effective in the field of mental health by applying insight from pastoral psychology to the major dimensions of the church's program. Contains a chapter on mental health and the group life of the church. (Originally published by Abingdon in 1965 under the title *Mental Health Through Christian Community*.)

Clinebell, Howard, Jr. *People Dynamic: Changing Self and Society Through Growth Groups.* New York: Harper and Row, 1972.

Gives many examples of the use of small groups in a variety of settings, including the church. The author is an outstanding leader in the field.

Coleman, Lyman. *Serendipity Books.* Waco, Texas: Creative Resources, 1971.

A series of person-centered "mini courses" based on self-discovery, process learning, and group dynamics. Includes Bible study and encounter techniques.

Driver, Helen, et al. *Counseling and Learning Through Small-Group Discussion.* Madison, Wisconsin: Monona-Drive Book Co., 1970.

Textbook in counseling and personal growth through small groups. Technical. Much attention to role playing as a technique.

Fast, Julius. *Body Language.* New York: M. Evans and Co., 1970.

How to read the signs we make with our bodies, revealing the unspoken inner feelings.

Freer, Harold, and Hall, Frances. *Two or Three Together.* New York: Harper and Row, 1954.

Subtitled "A Manual for Prayer Groups," this book is divided into two parts, the second half of which is a thirty-week series of "meditations and helps" for spiritual growth groups to use as a center for their thought and sharing. The first half of the book is an excellent discussion of the small group for prayer and sharing, how to begin, meet the problems, etc.

Gunther, Bernard. *Sense Relaxation Below Your Mind.* New York: Collier Books, 1968.

Instructions for sensitivity exercise alone, in groups, for married couples. Illustrated with photographs.

Haroutunian, Joseph. *God With Us: A Theology of Transpersonal Life.* Philadelphia: Westminster Press, 1965.

This book attempts to state a theology of relationship. The author says, "As a Christian, I may not forget that all the life I have with my fellowman is a life I have also with Christ."

Harris, Thomas, M.D. *I'm OK—You're OK: A Practical Guide to Transactional Analysis.* New York: Harper and Row, 1969.

A fresh approach to the Parent-Adult-Child concept made famous by Eric Berne in *Games People Play.* Helpful in understanding group interaction, especially conflict.

Howard, Jane. *Please Touch: A Guided Tour of the Human Potential Movement.* New York: McGraw-Hill Book Co., 1970.

Beginning as a lay person in the group movement, the author spent an entire year experiencing every type of sensitivity group from the extreme to the conventional all across the country.

Human Development Institute. *Basic Interpersonal Relations—A Course for Small Groups.* Atlanta: Bell & Howell, 1969.

A basic five-session course in interpersonal relations; booklets contain step by step instructions. To be used in a small (five to six persons) leaderless group.

Johnson, Ben. *Learning To Pray—A Guide for Beginner Groups.* Atlanta: Forum House, 1972.

In addition to guidelines for personal prayer, the author shares helpful insights which have enabled him to attain a more meaningful prayer experience. Simple guidance is given for beginning and continuing a prayer group.

Jones, E. Stanley. *A Song of Ascents.* Nashville: Abingdon Press, 1968.

The spiritual autobiography of the world-renowned author, missionary, and evangelist. Helpful in forming a theological foundation for encounter groups.

Kelly, Thomas. *A Testament of Devotion.* New York: Harper and Row, 1941.

One of the great books on the deeper spiritual life, blending the mystical and the practical. The author takes the reader along the path by which he has found his way into the presence of God, showing how one can lead a spiritual life in the world. Includes a biographical memoir of Kelly by Douglas Steere.

Killinger, John. *All You Lonely People, All You Lovely People*. Waco, Texas: Word, 1973.

A diary of the life and death of one small group. Provides priceless insights into the joys and sorrows of group involvement.

Knowles, Joseph. *Group Counseling*. Philadelphia: Fortress Press, 1967.

Small group advantages applied to specific problem-solving and counseling situations. Excellent help for pastor in how to introduce prayer therapy and group counseling into his church.

Leslie, Robert. *Sharing Groups in the Church*. Nashville: Abingdon Press, 1970.

Gives specific guidelines, many case studies, and examples for the development and clearly structured activity of sharing groups. Shows how small groups can function successfully with nonprofessional leadership.

Life That Really Matters, A. Tallahassee, Florida: Brave Christian Associates, 1965.

A description of the "John Wesley Great Experiment." It is the "autobiography of a corporate spiritual experience" and provides a plan for putting Christianity into practice via the group.

McMahon, Edwin, and Campbell, Peter. *Please Touch*. New York: Sheed and Ward, 1969.

Words and pictures, appealing to the sensitive person on the glory of God in "man fully alive," a wonderful expression of "incarnational theology" and how "love is the extension of God's community into the world, into us."

Malamud, Daniel, and Machover, Solomon. *Toward Self-Understanding: Group Techniques in Self-Confrontation*. Springfield, Illinois: Charles C. Thomas, 1970.

Workshops or encounter group sessions described with mental health clinic outpatients, illustrating role of leader, various group experiments, and member reactions. Interpretive commentaries added to workshop. Over sixty group experiments described.

Miller, Keith. *The Becomers.* Waco, Texas: Word, 1973.

Conversion is only the beginning, according to Keith Miller. From there one is a "becomer" in process, on the way toward deeper, more honest relationships with people, with God, and with oneself.

Oden, Thomas. *The Intensive Group Experience: The New Pietism.* Philadelphia: Westminster Press, 1972.

A critique and evaluation of the "encounter culture" developing around the encounter group movement. Provides an historical and theological analysis of the movement.

Olsen, Charles. *The Base Church.* Atlanta: Forum House, 1973.

Takes readers one step beyond the small group movement into alternative forms of Christian community. The author is director of Project Base Church for the Institute of Church Renewal.

Parker, William, and St. Johns, Elaine. *Prayer Can Change Your Life.* Englewood Cliffs, N.J.: Prentice-Hall, 1957.

One of the earliest experiments with self-honesty, using psychological testing for self-discovery in the context of a small supportive group. Prayer as a healing agent for personal wholeness and a practice of honesty is clinically explored.

Pfeiffer, J. W., and Jones, John. *A Handbook of Structured Experiences for Human Relations Training—Volumes 1—3.* Iowa City, Iowa: University Associates Publishers & Consultants, 1969.

A series of seventy-four games (in three paperback books) which encourage variation and creative use. Though the games need to be adapted, this is a helpful collection for a group leader. Permission is given for reproduction.

Powell, John. *Why Am I Afraid To Tell You Who I Am?* Chicago: Argus Communications, 1969.

A clearly stated discussion of the meaning of "encounter," with rules for accomplishing gut-level communication. Condensed explanation of the psychology of interpersonal relations.

Raines, Robert. *New Life in the Church.* New York: Harper and Row, 1961.

A pastor traces the renewal of life in his congregation and how this relates to the small fellowship group centering on Bible study, prayer, and honest sharing. Christian conversion takes place in the context of Christian fellowship (*koinonia*).

Reid, Clyde. *Groups Alive, Church Alive.* New York: Harper and Row, 1969.

Subtitled "The effective use of small groups in the local church." Nontechnical. Real life experiences show advantages and reasons for small groups and how many levels of interaction will be established for different groups in the same church.

Schutz, William. *Joy: Expanding Human Awareness.* New York: Grove Press, 1967.

A textbook on the theory and technique of interpersonal relations in encounter groups. This book is basic reading for those wishing to understand what "encounter" is all about, and for those desiring to be leaders of groups.

Udy, Gloster. *Key to Change.* Sydney, Australia: Donald Pettigrew, 1962.

Documentation of the small group fellowship as a Methodist class meeting movement; how the class meeting saved civilization at a time when society and the family were disintegrating, became a model for democracy, and is being rediscovered today in various forms to be a redemptive agent in our times.